This book can be toke-
nized. Scan the code to
claim the digital token.

"It's a story of inspiration, truly. Of sadness and joy, of growth and spirituality, and ultimately of acceptance. The blending of worlds, a seeming dichotomy that Carl has woven together into a spectacularly vibrant life. Reading his beautiful book has touched me deeply."

Barbara Manocherian
President—New York Stage and Film

"I first met Carl Moellenberg on the Broadway musical SPRING AWAKENING and we have worked together a number of times since. What a pleasure to read this memoir. It is full of heart, told with great honesty, in strong, clear, simple language. His fortitude and optimism in the face of adversity is an inspiration."

Tom Hulce
Actor/Producer

"Glorious, quiet power of hope throughout this beautiful, utterly relatable memoir reminds us to heed that inner ever present voice urging us onward. Exploding with simple wisdoms with those more complex matters of the heart subtly lurking between the lines."

Mary Beth O'Connor
RKO Pictures/ Lucky Viii Films

"Carl's story is one of finding profound passion in storytelling and bringing those stories to life. His memoir is searingly honest about his health struggles, but what stands out is how these challenges have consistently inspired him to live a fuller life; connect more deeply with people and work with the best artists to help deliver their vision. It's a lesson in defining one's life not by its challenges but by what -and who we love."

Tim Levy
Broadway and London Producer

"I am so honored Carl shared this very personal work with me. It is a beautiful experience to read. Not just because I consider Carl a friend, but because it is an exercise in authentic vulnerability, and the world needs so much more of that. If there's one thing his memoir showed me - or really, affirmed what I already knew about him - it's Carl's incredible Goodness, which I use with a capital G. He is one of the most pure, kind and Good people I have ever known. Carl's willingness to be so open and vulnerable around his survivorship, his spiritual path, his artistic path, and his close friendships allows the reader a sense of honor to be included in his journey.
I think this memoir can and will help people (in a universal sense) to feel less alone, and inspire them to follow themselves and their dreams."

Adam Kantor
Broadway actor

Carl Moellenberg's Story:

Broadway and Spirituality as a Path to Survival

CARL MOELLENBERG

Published by Imagine & Wonder
Irvington, New York 10533 USA
www.imagineandwonder.com

Cataloging-in-Publication information is available from the Library of Congress.

Library of Congress Control Number: 2021953226
ISBN: 9781637610466

First Edition

DEDICATION

To Chuck Moellenberg, Mark Stager, Bob Flicker, Michael Forsyth, Bobby Sain and Anthony Del Negro (in order of your coming into my life)

Without your bond and love, this professional and spiritual journey would never have happened.

FOREWORD

BY BOBBY SAIN

I met Carl Moellenberg in the summer of 2011. A mutual friend introduced us after I had produced my first film and taken an interest in being an entrepreneur. Carl and I had lunch at a Thai restaurant on 23rd Street where we bonded over a mutual love of good storytelling, sports, and the current events of the time—politics was always on the docket. My curiosity for building companies and telling meaningful stories went hand in hand with Carl's work. I was learning the ropes of film production as a newly minted twenty-five-year-old producer, and Carl was a veteran of investment banking and theater. I was looking for a mentor, and Carl was willing to take on a mentee. I got more than I bargained for as Carl and I soon became fast friends.

Over our many years of friendship, I have seen Carl's drive to finish the next play turn into a drive to develop his life's work: a portfolio of meaningful stories. He taught me the ropes of producing theater, encouraged me to chase my dreams as an entrepreneur, and introduced me to a group of wonderful people whom I still call friends to this day. Even though Carl's love of meaningful stories is his life's work, he has always said his love for meaningful friends makes that life enjoyable.

Carl hasn't had an easy life. After noticing Carl in an unusual amount of pain one day, from what seemed to be a relatively small issue, Carl sat me down and told me something he told few people: he is living life with HIV. As we worked together, I personally watched Carl endure the long-term effects of a forty-year battle with a terrible disease.

In the 1980s HIV tore through New York City, killing thousands, while the city turned its back on an entire community of people. Carl was not spared. I do not know what it was like to be a gay man in the 1980s; all I know is that it wasn't easy. Society marginalized these American citizens, and HIV added insult to injury.

In Carl's time, a newly diagnosed HIV patient was lucky to see their next birthday. Through Carl's tenacity and good fortune, he has now seen forty birthdays since his diagnosis. He has shown the world, and, more importantly, himself that HIV was just an unfortunate pit stop on the road trip to pursuing his dreams. After nearly dying of AIDS, Carl found a silver lining resulting from many spiritual practices he had taken on. Two life-changing experiences described in the memoir happened before I met him, but they were astounding. He made the decision to save his life by leaving the drain of investment banking behind and pursuing his life's passion: the theater.

Being a producer can mean a lot of different things. To Carl, it meant telling stories. Many of us know that life has an expiration date. Carl had it rubber-stamped on an official document, and storytelling was the one thing that made him feel alive. With this new lease on life, Carl didn't pull a punch; he was part of creating some of the most meaningful theatrical productions of the last twenty years—shows that have drawn in millions and have won countless awards. And at the center of it all were thought-provoking and inspiring messages. His perseverance to stay alive was in no small part due to his love of the theater. I have personally seen him many times in very difficult circumstances due to the long-term side effects of HIV and multiple pulmonary embolisms. His love of theater, and ultimately his love of story, moved into producing films, documentaries, and other staged stories for audiences to enjoy—he had found his passion.

I count myself lucky to have met Carl. He has been a personal mentor and guide to me. He has given me advice when I have made mistakes, listened to me when I have gone through difficult times, and supported my work as an entrepreneur. He will tell me when I am failing but will be there for me, so I don't fully fall. In addition to being someone I trust with the most important parts of my life, Carl has been my friend. I hope reading Carl's memoir inspires you the way Carl's battle and friendship have inspired me.

I am one of the many that have had the good fortune to know Carl Moellenberg. Carl's determination through struggle is an inspiration to me. Carl wrote this memoir in hopes of inspiring many more.

—Bobby Sain

INTRODUCTION

For many years, I've had wonderful friends who were constantly prodding me to write a story about my life. I don't view anything about myself as extraordinary. I also know so many people are dealing with debilitating health issues, as I have over 40 years. My friends believe I might be able to provide inspiration to others by sharing my personal journey. There is a lot to share. Part of me is terrified at my life literally becoming an "open book," and I hope you support my genuine reason for doing so. These experiences have created the person I am today. This is my life story—one of resilience, transformation, perseverance, surviving, adapting, healing, spirituality, love, faith, finding my passion and realizing dreams. It is a story about facing daunting obstacles head on and not losing hope.

—Carl

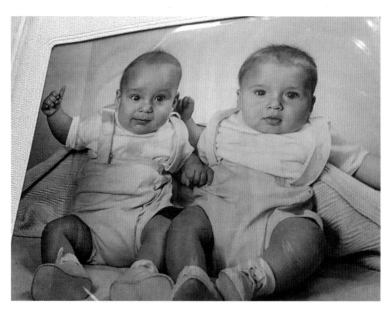

Baby Brothers

ACT ONE

THE NEST

"Let's start at the very beginning. A very good place to start."
—*The Sound of Music*

L et's start at the very beginning—really, the very beginning. The set: my mother's womb. My parents had been trying to have a child for many years, and they were ecstatic to have a baby on the way nine years after marrying. Delivery day arrives, but I don't seem to be moving. Instead, my brother emerges as a healthy boy. Then, the doctor suddenly announces that another baby is on the way—they had *no* idea they were having twins!

Five minutes later I tumbled out backwards. Was this an omen for how the rest of my life would be? My parents were elated but also shocked. They only had one name chosen, which was Carl, after my paternal grandfather. Even though I was the second arrival, they gave me that name and made my brother a Charles Jr.

My parents were off to buy doubles of everything and decided they were done with this baby making thing.

Chuck and Carl

IS THIS REALLY NECESSARY?

Although we are fraternal twins and not identical, we looked quite a bit alike through at least age eight. Our parents made the decision to dress us exactly the same up until kindergarten. We also were placed in the same kindergarten class. As a result, we were lumped together in everyone's minds and not seen as individuals.

I still remember the first day of kindergarten. I refused to come out from the coatroom and was crying nonstop. Mom would not leave me alone in there, and she and the teacher were taking a cautious path toward convincing me it was okay to come out. Then all of a sudden this rather brazen little girl named Cynthia came in and kissed me right on the mouth. It definitely stopped me from crying, and as it was my first kiss, I did not know what to make of it.

Eventually, I emerged into the real world and sat at a desk. A week later, the principal called my parents in and said not to dress my brother and me alike anymore (thank God!), and that we would not be placed in the same class in future years.

At this age, our most differentiating characteristic was that I have blue eyes and my brother's are brown. The unusual blue eyes I inherited from my mother would turn out to play a major role in my life. Later on, I realized that the combination of the soft blue color, coupled with my always looking right at people with direct eye contact, had one of two effects. For some people, they would say my eyes were penetrating, and I seemed to be looking right through them; they were uncomfortable. Fortunately, many more people said I had beautiful warm eyes that made them feel heard, welcomed, and embraced. It was a kind of power, but not a manufactured one—rather, a natural benefit that caused others to speak their truth to me and to seek me out for advice.

We can do casual too lol

REALIZING MY NAME IS BOTH
CARL AND CHUCK

The toughest part of being a twin is being grouped together as one person. I was called Chuck very often and learned to turn my head to that name also. I remember wanting people to realize that we had our own likes and dislikes, friends, talents and weaknesses. But we also seemed to always be together.

The nicest part of being a twin was always having someone to play sports with. It could be plastic golf ball holes, basketball on a garage hoop, football, wiffle ball—you name it. Every game was a ferocious and fun competition with us.

It has been said many times that twins have a much stronger link than regular siblings, and this was very true for us. We had an unspoken understanding that is difficult to describe. We could virtually read each other's minds. We were co-conspirators in the game of being present and polite but not speaking up when guests were over. We were the "presentable" twins. We kind of felt like we were being shown off, but not expected to express an opinion or show emotions. Just smile and be polite.

I have often wondered how this stronger bond between twins happens. Is it simply because we are constantly together and the same age? Is it genetic? Is it because we are drawn to look out for the other more intensely than other siblings?

My third-grade classroom

EARLY AMBITION AND MY TEACHERS

From a very early age, it was ingrained in us by our parents to be the very best. Although it was not explicitly stated, I always felt tremendous pressure to excel and to please my parents.

My parents were extremely proud of us early on. They taught us to be well-behaved, to listen and to respect others. Beyond that though, there was a mostly unspoken expectation that we would do all our homework first before anything else, to fit into the family life pattern out of school and to get the highest grades or marks always. I was terrific at taking tests, so that was not a problem, but I was always very quiet in class from kindergarten all through grad school.

I can remember my first real challenge as a student. It was the summer before third grade, and Mrs. Munn announced a contest for all her students. We were to read as many books as possible before school started and write a short report on the book in a format that could fit on an index card. The person who wrote the most acceptable book reports would get a free movie night with popcorn and candy.

I was not going to lose this contest under any circumstances! Even at the age of eight, I was a voracious reader. I *read* and read and read through the summer and submitted nearly ninety book reports. Needless to say, no one was remotely close to that number, so I could have slacked off a bit!

I still remember the movie night, and it was a great reward! Mrs. Munn turned out to be my favorite teacher. All through grade school she was always there to support and encourage this overly ambitious little boy. She and my mom also became very close. For me, she has always been the epitome of what an encouraging teacher can be.

Me and my piano

MISS BLANCHARD SCARED ME

Our parents started us on piano lessons at a young age. Although it seemed to be a burden at the time, it fostered my love of music, which remained and shaped the rest of my life. Our teacher, Miss Blanchard, was a very short and demanding lady who always positioned herself right next to us at lessons, making sure we sat ramrod straight and used appropriate hand technique. If we hadn't practiced enough before the lesson, we were rebuked rather sternly.

Taking lessons each year culminated in the annual recital event, which was held in a very large hall at the Toledo Library. All her students had to participate in front of a large audience of friends and family. The students were arranged from the least advanced to the most advanced. One by one we got up and walked up the steps to the baby grand piano on a stage. It was terrifying to me!

We took lessons from Miss Blanchard all the way through high school. In the last year, I had the honor of being placed last in the program as the most advanced student that she showed off to parents and prospective new students. I was playing two pieces by memory, and my biggest fear was simply forgetting them in my terror, which remained even at age seventeen. Sure enough, I started the first piece (Debussy) and played the first line once, twice, three times without stopping until I remembered what was next. From there, it was smooth sailing.

After my performance, she cornered me and said I had her really scared. She was sure I was going to walk off the stage after ten seconds. But she was proud of me!

The piano lessons and the singing through high school were important influences in my life, and I am so glad my parents pushed us to stay with it. Music ultimately led to some major life decisions and is one of my true loves. And all these years later, I have this piano in my living room.

"We would start off with Lassie at seven p.m., then Ed Sullivan at eight and finally Bonanza at nine."

SUNDAY NIGHTS AT GRANDPA MOE'S

Our Sunday night tradition meant a family gathering at my dad's parents' house. Grandpa Moe, as he was affectionately nick-named, would be in his armchair, smoking his pipe. And he always had one of his three succession of dachshunds at his feet. They were always named Trinka, and they would attack us if we went anywhere near him.

Grandpa was a friendly man, but it was a bit hard to get to know him well. In addition to the attack dachshund protecting him, he was a man of few words. He was very proud of his large family, and that was always clear.

The kitchen at Grandpa Moe's was always the center of the gatherings because this is where we all played cards...and this is where the food and drinks were kept. The games would vary depending on the number of people playing, but rummy was most prevalent. Card playing was a huge part of our immediate family and my extended family on both sides.

In the living room, Sunday nights had the best schedule of TV shows for boys my age. We would start off with Lassie at seven p.m., then Ed Sullivan at eight and finally Bonanza at nine. We would be glued to the tube for all three shows. The highlight of course was the Beatles, first appearing on Ed Sullivan and then capturing America.

Even though Sunday night had this great family gathering and terrific TV watching, it also meant that tomorrow we were back in school. It was the "there is school tomorrow morning" pit in my stomach. Sunday nights were bittersweet because of that. We were doing fine in school, but there was always a pressure underlying our achievements.

"This was the ultimate in being nerds, I know, but we kind of owned our nerdship."

MY EARLY FRIENDSHIPS

My brother and I had a small group of boys that we hung out with in the limited hours that we were allowed to be away from home or school. Our activities initially revolved around collecting stamps and trading and researching new ones. We had books filled with stamps from countries around the world. This was the ultimate in being nerds, I know, but we kind of owned our nerdship. It was a small "band of brothers" that made us happy, and this was the most carefree time that I can remember.

I should also point out that we were pretty physically active as we also played football in the empty streets or yards. I don't remember any of us being particularly talented or particularly bad either. It was clear early on that we were not destined for any varsity teams in high school. In addition to the lack of talent, we were too short.

It occurs to me that we also were very concerned about being accepted and about what others said about us. My parents were, not surprisingly, the same way. My dad felt unappreciated at work and at golf and struggled to be one of the guys. My mom felt shortchanged by being a full-time mom when she was so smart. Part of their gaining acceptance was bragging about how well we were doing in school. We learned from their behavior to be extra sensitive to being liked, as opposed to just being ourselves.

1965 Palm Sunday Tornadoes. A wide outbreak of 37 tornadoes killed 256 people, mostly in Ohio, Michigan and Indiana on Palm Sunday 1965. The only tornado on April 11 to touch down in a large city hit Toledo at about 9:30 PM. It cut a six-mile-long path across the northern edge of Toledo.

Newspaper coverage on April 17th, 1965

THE DAY A TORNADO LITERALLY UPROOTED OUR LIVES

That was from a national story about the tornado which hit our house. We were home, except Dad who had taken our grandma home after a Sunday dinner. He made it back home with thirty seconds to spare, and we yelled for him to come right to the basement because he was unaware of the warnings. If you have never had the experience, I can tell you that tornados definitely do sound like freight trains. It hit our house and neighborhood with a tremendous frightening force.

When we felt it was safe, we went upstairs in the dark to survey the damage. It was pitch black as the power was gone, and peering out the window, we weren't sure what we were seeing. It turned out that pieces of the stores from the mall a few blocks away had flown sharply into our yard and were wedged everywhere. Our house was brick, but there was still extensive damage; live power lines were dangling dangerously all around the house and street. It was hard to figure out in the dark what everything was, but in the morning, the extent of the damage was overwhelming. We moved to our grandmother's house temporarily to avoid the downed lines and shrapnel from the mall.

Over the next several days, we witnessed our house and our neighborhood on national newscasts. Dad was continuously haggling with the insurance company; it turned out we were not in "good hands." Our house had such significant damage that it only made sense to move, so right before junior high school we left all our friends behind for a different school district. It is a tough time to arrive unknown among kids who had known each other all their school lives. We were now in a suburb of Toledo called Sylvania.

The first time I ever really felt like an outcast happened when we arrived in the new school district. My initial reaction was to withdraw even further into myself to not be singled out or made fun of. It took until mid-sophomore year in high school to begin to feel more accepted and to have new close friends. I finally found a group of people with similar interests with whom I could bond.

Me with Dad and Mom at our house

THE CHECKLIST FOR A TYPICAL MIDWESTERNER'S HOME

Y ou could easily say that my family home looked just like any midwestern setting right out of any 1950s–60s television show about life in the suburbs.

✓ Ranch style structure
✓ Burnt orange shag carpeting
✓ Twin boys sharing a bedroom with twin beds
✓ Big back yard for any kind of sports plus a basketball hoop
✓ Mom preparing dinner, which was served at 5:30 every weeknight – meatloaf or chicken breast or tuna noodle casserole, her "specialties" ....
✓ Dad coming home from work in time for a family meal then...

Oops...what could disrupt that pattern? Well, occasionally Dad would go out for drinks after work with his office mates and get home later than 5:30. He would try to pretend he had been working late. Unfortunately, he had a tell. If he had too many drinks, he would start sneezing non-stop. My brother and I made a game of it. We would count each sneeze at the dinner table while Mom glared at Dad.

His record was 122! Did this make for a calm and pleasant meatloaf dinner? Um…. no!

But other than that, we could have been a smaller Midwestern TV family with our predictable patterns.

Ohio State Hoodie

WATCHING SPORTS CONSUMED
OUR FAMILY TIME

M om was anything but the stereotypical "housewife." She had little interest in cooking or women's groups, but rather had been a good athlete in her past. She still loved to play tennis and golf, and our time at home was spent cheering on our college and professional teams across the spectrum of sports. She was one of the boys.

Of course, at the top of the list was THE Ohio State Buckeyes. *Almost* everyone in the state of Ohio idolized the Buckeyes. My parents attended the Ohio State–Michigan football games in person with another couple for decades, even sitting through blizzards. I did say *almost* everyone, except for my mom. She rooted for Michigan, which was taboo.

It was so much fun that we all loved sports! We lived very close to the Michigan state line, so all our favorite pro teams were in Detroit: the Red Wings (hockey), Pistons (basketball), Lions (football), and for baseball, of course we loved the Tigers…. We went up to Tiger Stadium pretty often, and that was always a highlight.

My Detroit Tigers book

THE 1968 DETROIT TIGERS SAVED THE CITY

T he 1968 Tigers were playing in the midst of terrible national race riots after the assassination of Martin Luther King on April 4, 1968. Detroit had already been struggling mightily as a city, and the riots tore the city apart.

Cheering on the Tigers who ultimately won the World Series against the St Louis Cardinals unified the city. I don't think I missed listening to or watching a single game all season as they won 103 games. Al Kaline was my boyhood idol; he could do it all. Denny McLain won thirty-one games and the Cy Young Award. Mickey Lolich was the hero of the World Series (three complete game wins) and a beloved blue-collar pitcher with a beer belly. The team was filled with personalities and talents that made me strive to know every fact about every player.

There have been many books and movies and documentaries about how this victorious season essentially inspired the residents of Detroit and surrounding areas to have hope. It brought them a common cause and a resiliency, no matter how hurting everyone was from the tragedy around them. I'll never forget that year, and to this day I can tell you about the entire team... Mickey Stanley, Jim Northrup, Bill Freehan, Gates Brown, and others may not be household names, but they live vividly in my memory.

"But it's all a game, right? Ummmm—not when we played."

FAMILY GOLF OUTINGS AND NEEDLING
MY BROTHER UNTIL HE CRACKED

Our most frequent family outing was as a foursome playing golf at Sylvania Country Club, a rather demanding course. We made a motley family group. My dad desperately wanted to be a good player to be accepted by his peers at the club, but never conquered a wicked slice. He spent the day looking for balls in the right woods. He was always looking at the group behind us and worrying we were holding them up. My mom was five feet tall but hit the ball a long way when she connected.

My brother and I were of course very competitive, and each hated losing to the other. There was no doubt my brother had the better swing and form and was a longer hitter. He was clearly the better golfer. My specialty was chipping around the greens and hitting the ball straight.

Chuck would usually get off to a nice lead over me, but I was always biding my time. I knew that if he had one bad hole it could lead to several bad holes in a row. Why? First, he had a terrible temper with himself; he would start shouting obscenities and even throw his clubs in the creek. All of this horrified my parents as they wondered how many other club members were observing this and judging us. Second, I discovered small ways to needle him after he started the decline, which would prolong it. For me, it was a calculated psychological attrition that would allow me often to win despite being less talented. But it's all a game, right? Ummmm—not when we played.

Mom's parents

Family picnic with Dad's side of the family

THE PURITANS VERSUS THE ROWDIES

Our families on my mom's side versus my dad's side could not have been more different. You can probably figure out which one I easily preferred.

My mom was from an extended family of many farming relatives, although her immediate family members were not. In addition to the simple life of rising early and reclining early, many were also teetotalers. Some were members of the Women's Christian Temperance Union, although not my mom. Most of them were Methodists, and we were raised in the Methodist Church. I saw no real spirituality there; it seemed like a social gathering to show off their new clothes or new jobs. Large family reunions were painful as we did not fit in and did not know what to say and had never raised a crop or milked a cow. More immediate family gatherings were simply not exciting. Again, we sat and were not heard primarily.

On the other hand, my dad's side loved to party. They were devout Catholics from many nationalities through marriage. The Moellenbergs were originally from southern Germany. Marriage brought a really fun, Irish, red-headed arm to the family, and they loved their beers. Family gatherings were a blast, and Dad always made a punch that was so spiked that his older sisters were wobbling down the driveway at the end of the night. Everyone loved to laugh and make jokes at each other's expense. I remember going out with my cousins later in life for many beers and sneaking home to my parents' place while supposedly "quietly" ransacking their liquor cabinet and getting caught. The family also had a cottage on a lake in Michigan that hosted probably my favorite childhood events. Card games, going out in the lake, great food that everyone brought up, and the Tigers on TV. Heaven!

"My parents were very competitive too, and of course my brother and I went at it, life or death."

THREE OTHER FAMILY TRADITIONS

Every Sunday we grilled steaks outside and had salad and tater tots. Dinner was usually around two p.m., and I think about it all the time even now. Often on special occasions I re-enact that meal and think of my parents. I *love* steaks as a result of that tradition and even search out places that have tater tots on the menu. Very high cuisine!

Another family hobby was playing card games of all types. The most frequent were rummy, gin, euchre, poker, bridge and pinochle. This went on within our nuclear four-person family, but also when we were with extended family or friends of my parents. My favorite one was the most obscure—pinochle—which was the game of choice of my grandmother on my mom's side. She would get out her famous cardholders of all colors, and we would go at it. We would be treated afterward by her concoction of lime Jell-O and cottage cheese mixed together.

I was able to remember cards that had been played, had a really complete grasp of strategy, was risky, and could read people's faces. Pinochle especially was my game to win. As a result, my parents often said they should send me to Las Vegas. I really miss having people to play cards with in NYC; it seems to be more a Midwestern habit. If we weren't eating or watching sports, we were likely playing cards in our spare time.

We had a ping pong table in our basement, and ping pong family matches were always pretty ferocious, either in singles or doubles. My parents were very competitive too, and of course my brother and I went at it, life or death. Unlike golf at that time, we were all pretty good at this, and most people visiting us from outside of the family could not beat us. A measure of satisfaction...

"My dating life will not take long to describe."

DATING...SORT OF

My dating life will not take long to describe. I had isolated dates with about four girls, which were very innocent—dinners, movies, putt-putt golf. I'm not even sure I could pick out a highlight. My very first fooling around was with a wild girl on the front lawn of her house after I dropped her off at her mom's house very late one night. A few years later when I came home for summer vacation from college, *her mom* asked me over and wanted to have sex. Her daughter had joined the Navy. Ummmmm… no.

Then there was also the movie date when my date could not handle watching a little violence and proceeded to vomit in my lap… Yea – good times!

When it came to the senior prom, there was a lot of pressure from all sides to go and have the "perfect time." My parents were, of course, all in, and everyone at school was busy asking everyone who they were going with. I asked a girl who was very pretty and probably above my league, so to speak, but miracle of miracles she said yes. We went shopping for tuxedos, and of course, I picked out an all gold one (*don't even ask!*). I would show you the picture, but I destroyed the evidence.

Then only a few days before the prom, she dumped me and was going with someone else. I was humiliated and locked myself in the bathroom at home and refused to come out. There was no way I was going to prom now with everyone knowing my "disgrace." Meanwhile, as Mom was trying everything to get me out of the bathroom over quite an extended period of time, she also was finding me a date. She arranged for me to go with another girl while I was still in the bathroom. I was still not happy, but she saved the day as she did so many times over her life.

Mom The Fixer

MY MOM WAS "THE FIXER"

Mom was the "go to" person for so many family members, both within our immediate family and within our extended family. She was the person who listened to the problem and figured out how to fix it. An earlier day Olivia Pope!

I could name countless family members who came to my mom for help in many different forms. Her support might be in the form of advice or in action steps or in providing money when others were in need. She was a very good listener and a terrific problem solver. She came to the rescue of *many* family members, even when their immediate family members could or wouldn't help.

Mom was the most giving person I have ever met and had a huge heart. At the same time, she could be very outspoken and created animosities along the way. Because of that, she often did not get the credit she was due for holding her side of the family together in many very difficult situations.

Quiz Bowl with me and my brother

SINGING AND SCHOLARSHIP

In addition to continuing piano lessons, my brother and I both loved singing. Our high school had a beloved director of choral programs whom we all loved and respected tremendously. Chorus practice, unlike piano practice, was always a joy. The chorus had a great reputation and did very well in competitions. The combination of having extended piano and singing in my life for years had become something I realized needed to be a part of my life forever.

Meanwhile, the Moellenberg twins continued to do well academically. We were on the high school televised Quiz Bowl team. Everyone laughed at our nameplates, since they could not fit Moellenberg. We were Carl M'berg and Chuck M'berg, which of course became a nickname. In the continued keeping of being twins, we were nominated as a joint entity to be Scholars of the Year, when every other nominee was an individual. It never stopped, but the novelty of having the twins on the ballot linked probably helped us win.

I never felt that I really fit in at high school after our late move to the area following the tornado. High school was a fairly low point in life for a number of reasons. I also think I was starting to realize that I might be different.

Mom and Dad

LEAVING THE NEST

It was time to leave the cozy confines of home and head off to college. Mom cried a lot (rumors that I did too are unsubstantiated).

I really had not begun to discover who I was. I was modeling myself after what others wanted me to be. When I think back to my "personhood" at that time, it brings several adjectives to mind:

- Naive
- Innocent
- Over-protected
- Sheltered
- Ambitious
- Competitive
- Sensitive
- Eager to be liked
- Kind but not spiritual (so far)
- Scared and excited
- Bright but not philosophical (yet)
- Honest
- Giving
- Listener rather than talker

I was a blank slate ready to discover, learn, but most importantly, experience the camaraderie and friendships of a college campus. I feel blessed to have loving, caring parents, but also stifled by their keeping us so confined. I didn't know who I was on my own. That was soon to change—the 70s of self-discovery and exploration were ahead!

ACT TWO

NOT A NEST, BUT STILL AN OASIS

ONE MOMENT IN TIME ... sung by Whitney Houston and written by John Bettis and Albert Hammond

Each day I live
I want to be
A day to give
The best of me
I'm only one
But not alone
My finest day
Is yet unknown

I want one moment in time
Where I'm more than I thought I could be
When all of my dreams are a heartbeat away
And the answers are all up to me

Give me one moment in time
When I'm racing with destiny
Then in that one moment in time
I will feel
I will feel eternity

Denison University

DENISON UNIVERSITY THE IDYLLIC COLLEGE ON A HILL

I was accepted into several more prominent eastern colleges but decided to go to Denison University in Ohio for several reasons. When I visited, it was a stunning, small campus with about 2,000 students. Everyone seemed to be very friendly, and it had a strong liberal arts reputation. Class sizes were small, and I liked the possibility of building close friends and participating in so many activities. Honestly, at that time I also wanted to be closer to home, having been so sheltered previously. I was only cautiously out of the cocoon. Denison was in a tiny town named Granville, about a forty-five-minute drive from Columbus and a two-hour drive from Toledo.

My brother also had applied and been accepted to many schools, some overlapping with mine and some not. Our parents made us put our first choices into a hat without consulting each other. He picked Denison too. This wound up causing a complicated set of reactions during our four years there, as you can imagine. We packed up our bags and arrived at the freshman dorm for orientation week. Denison turned out to be the perfect choice and among the happiest years in my life. I would turn the clock back and return to college in a heartbeat if I could!

"Ultimately, I wound up as co-valedictorian, summa cum laude, and my parents were happy. But college was so much more than that. I was not a geek… really!"

I WAS NOT A GEEK!

It was incredible to be able to take the full diversity of classes offered by a liberal arts school. I savored philosophy, economics, psychology, political science, mathematics, piano, voice, literature—you name it. As I had hoped, both fellow students and teachers were very friendly and made academics fun. We talked about topics that were universal and far-ranging, which I had never even considered before. I think this diversity of studies is so important to an education—to get an introduction to the classics and the masters in their fields and to be able to dig deeper when one discussion really intrigues you. I wound up using psychology and philosophy way more in life than calculus!

I was driven to excel and always found school easy. I often wished I could just be a professional student and somehow make a living that way – ha-ha! I loved to write, and most exams were handwritten in "blue books" they handed out… small pamphlets. I had the advantage of being able to write very fast and to the point with perfect spelling, grammar, and structure that had been taught and ingrained in me. At several points in school, I wished I could just be a student forever!

Ultimately, I wound up as co-valedictorian, summa cum laude, and my parents were happy. But college was so much more than that. I was not a geek…. really!

Some of my fraternity brothers

FRATERNITY BONDING

Fraternities were very big on campus, and rush began in the second semester of freshman year. Of course, with every college, some fraternities were known as the jock houses, the party houses, the rich kids, the heavy hazing ones, and so on. I had no chance at those but wanted to join one to experience the bonding of a brotherhood. There was one lesser-known house named Delta Chi, which did not have jocks or the most popular guys, but rather was more an academic fraternity with nice guys who all probably had no other choices other than remaining independent. I decided to join with a group of my friends from the freshman dorm, and it was the best decision of college. This was when I realized how important very personal friendships would always be in my life.

It's hard to describe how close you can become with living together and having each other's backs for the next three years. We hung out together, ate meals together, studied, went out drinking, played sports against other fraternities, planned frat activities, and became lifelong friends in some cases. It was my first exhilarating time being on my own and having freedom to do what I wanted, along with finding great people to hang out with. Better late than never, as they say.

Fraternity moment (beers!)

THE BEST OF TIMES

The experiences with my fraternity brothers might have been the best time of my life. There are so many, and I need to give you a flavor of them:

We competed in every intramural sport, but we totally sucked. We had no true jocks, were undermanned, but tried really hard.

- There was the day our best athlete was late to a softball game, and we saw him running down the hill to join us as we were mockingly yelling that it was a close game and to get his ass here fast. When he arrived, he learned we were already losing by 23-0.

- There were our touch football games where we were smaller and less talented. I had one game playing middle linebacker at 5'8", 130. Shortly into the game, a receiver came barreling at me, and his shoulder at high speed collided with my mouth. I lost three teeth to root canals, had a crazy looking swollen lip, and was sipping milkshakes out of a straw for weeks. So much for being the next Nick Butkus. That was my last game at that position.

- Also in football, we had a somewhat loudmouth guy who insisted he could kick a field goal rather than us going for a touchdown. We lined up, he stepped back to kick the FG and proceeded to kick a line drive right into our center's butt. No one could stop laughing (other than the center).

- There were our basketball games where we were somewhat competitive and had the added benefit of inheriting a 6'4" foreign exchange student from Argentina. Unfortunately, his single game strategy was running down the court screaming *"Give me ball. I score."* Literally. The entire opponent's team collapsed around him, and he didn't score very often.

- We were better at sports where there was one person or two people rather than having to field a whole team. Guess what our best "sport" was? PING PONG, OF COURSE! My brother and I had been playing doubles together for years, and we did great. He had a lethal forehand, and I had an awesome backhand holding my paddle like most Asian players. The question, you may ask, is whether ping pong is a sport.

But sports were not everything. Our frat was the very best at blaring Beach Boys music out every window each Friday afternoon while throwing frisbees. Beach Boys are the happiest "live and let live" music ever written. Pure carefree bliss.

We usually would follow that up by driving into Newark, Ohio (pronounced by the locals as 'Nerk') for beers at the Stein. The campus and town of Granville were dry, and so we had to join the townies of 'Nerk' who did not much appreciate our company. Many pitchers later we would tumble back into our cars, me usually lying in the back seat comatose. Another guess challenge: what was our go to drink other than beers? I bet you didn't guess and may not have even heard of Singapore Slings. They were red and very sweet... that is all.

We were not a big hazing house, but our annual largest event was putting a scavenger list together that the pledges had twenty-four hours to complete. Some were risqué items but still pretty tame. Our biggest doofus and life-threatening debacle was dropping a weighted dummy from a Piper Cherokee plane into a field. Instead of going down, the dummy went straight back and tangled itself around the rudder of the plane. The plane was flying erratically, and we deliberately landed on a runway as far from the Controller of the small airport as possible while we scrambled to get it off the back of the plane. No one died.

"We were kind of a fraternity that was an anti-fraternity fraternity. A motley collection of guys who bonded in the best of ways. We were there for each other."

The 1972-73 Denison Singers.

Four Events

Denison Singers Highlight Concert Sch

Denison Singers

MUSIC AT DENISON

I was still taking piano lessons during the whole time there. But the other major bonding experience of college was singing in three different sized choral groups. One was a 100-person concert choir, another a forty-person church choir and the last a fifteen-person a cappella group called imaginatively The Singers.

The Singers group was difficult to get into and well known in the Midwest. Our director was very demanding and put together very difficult programs. I sang first tenor, and we performed on campus and toured throughout the U.S. Most of the music was classical, often madrigal. Touring made for fantastic adventures with fellow singers and some amazing venues at which to perform. My favorite probably was the National Cathedral where the acoustics were so good you could sing sotto voce and hear it echo through the vast space.

I have always loved singing classical music and working to conquer demanding material as a group. The practices were tough, but the exhilaration afterward and the camaraderie, especially traveling together, made it more than worthwhile.

"I was beginning to realize, but not to acknowledge, that I was attracted to guys."

DATING VERSUS BEST FRIEND

I was still dating girls occasionally, but it just did not compare to hanging out with my closest friends. I was beginning to realize, but not to acknowledge, that I was attracted to guys. I had no gay role models in Ohio in an earlier generation where people did not come out early. I did not act out on it at all.

But there was no question that my first (unrequited) love was the handsome, smart, and incredibly nice, best athlete in our fraternity. I wanted nothing more than to be in his company. We went to mass together and that was my first time going to a Catholic church every Sunday. He was bright and kind and fun loving—and also his girlfriend was at a different campus. He was completely straight, and sexuality never came up because I had not even addressed it in my own mind. I remember being in agony when his girlfriend visited for a weekend.

I was really attracted to everything about him, and it kind of consumed me. I had never had a friend like this before, and I had never realized my attraction to a guy before, much less one this strong. However, he was never in my mind anything other than a best friend.

I never said anything about how intense my feelings were; we just hung out together and were pretty inseparable. In retrospect, this was my first love—unacknowledged, unspoken—and experienced only through an amazing friendship. The first love is never forgotten and holds a special place in my heart.

Graduation Day (*It was the '70s.*)

LEAVING DENISON BEHIND

I left a totally different person than four years prior. I felt proud of the academic achievements (co-valedictorian), but those were not on the top of my mind. I felt like I could talk about so many topics that I previously knew nothing about. I had experienced bonding and closeness as never before, whether through the fraternity or singing. It still was a bit of a cocoon on top of a hill in Ohio, but I was more well-rounded and adjusted to deal with what was to lie ahead.

Most of all though I was sad. Inconsolably sad. I didn't want to leave this place that I cherished. It was a magical place and not the real world. I didn't want to say goodbye to the friends I had made and with whom I had experienced so many crazy times together. But I especially wanted to stay with my best friend, and that was impossible. Law school was ahead for him and business school for me, geographically apart, but a relationship I will never forget. As I write this so many years later, the tears are streaming down my cheeks, as they were when we said goodbye and through most of the summer afterward.

Acceptance letter from Harvard

Acceptance letter from University of Chicago

BUSINESS SCHOOL IS A WHOLE DIFFERENT ANIMAL

My parents really wanted me to get a business degree foundation for long term financial reasons. I wasn't even sure business was the field I wanted to pursue. I knew I loved music but what would I do to make a living there?

At the time I was applying to business schools, there were three schools very clearly at the top of the rankings: Harvard, University of Chicago, and Stanford. I applied to all three, plus other good schools as backups. I was pleasantly surprised to get accepted at Harvard and Chicago right out of undergrad with no work experience.

The decision was not actually very tough. Chicago offered me a full scholarship, while Harvard offered no aid. Chicago was analytically oriented and had the best reputation in finance, while Harvard emphasized oral arguments. I did not want my parents to have to put up more money when I had a full ride to a great school. Chicago also played to my strengths, and I thought I would do better there, although one could argue that I could have bolstered my weakness of public speaking by going to Harvard.

I decided to attend Chicago, and it was sneakily kind of cool to say no to Harvard. Arriving at the Gothic environment on the dangerous south side of Chicago was a totally different animal than the first day at Denison. It felt somewhat foreboding as opposed to gorgeous and friendly. I also immediately recognized that most of my classmates were high achievers and very competitive. The classes were extremely challenging from day one and very serious in their delivery. They meant business, literally.

University of Chicago campus

CHICAGO IS ALSO VERY DIFFERENT FROM GRANVILLE

Chicago Business School was a very different animal and environment from Denison. There was much less time for camaraderie, and it was much more serious. It was very hard work, but, in the end, I finished again at the top of the class with an MBA in finance. At Denison and at Chicago, I had all A's except for one B during the years there, but so many times I thought I had done terribly immediately after taking any test.

Chicago was the first large city for me; it had so much to offer when we did have spare time. Rush Street was a maze of bar after bar. I developed an absolute love of deep-dish pizza at Gino's.

We were advised to be very cautious walking even a few blocks away from the oasis of campus for safety reasons. I developed a few core friends who remain friends to this day. I also had another straight guy who was my good friend and partner in crime there, too. But life there did not have the joy of Denison by a long shot, and that is probably why I have little to say about those two years. They happened; I did well so that I had a wide choice of offers in several cities and different types of firms.

It still was school though and not the real world. That reality weighed on me. I knew academics suited me, but would business? Plus, my real love had always been music, and that would no longer be part of my life. Would I like the real world? I knew I could thrive in an academic environment; being tossed into a bank as an analyst was an entirely different challenge.

"I sat down in the reclining desk chair, leaned back, and it completely tipped over backwards with me flying over the chair and landing in a crazy position on the floor."

JOB CHOICES AFTER COLLEGE

I was lucky to have a lot of job offers, but this also brought a lot of complications. The offers spanned the fields of management consulting, banking, investment banking, rotating trainee programs in industrial corporations, and a small think tank group.

The cities involved were very different too—Chicago, New York City, San Francisco, Toledo, Dallas. I was hoping also to room with a close friend from school as I entered the business world.

I ultimately decided, after changing my mind a few times, to go with the small think tank. I was joining a group of seven very high-level people at Chemical Bank in New York City, including the president of the bank and people who later would be the CFO, the treasurer, the head of asset/liability management, etc. We were to tackle what the president decided were projects of importance to the bank overall. We met first thing every morning for brainstorming and bank/industry/project discussion. I decided I would learn the most here, but it was high risk given these were among the smartest people in the bank with major experience, and I was their first-time guinea pig straight from school.

It was also my very first job. As I walked in, I met everyone, and they showed me my office, which I would share with one other person. You couldn't make up what happened next. I sat down in the reclining desk chair, leaned back, and it completely tipped over backwards with me flying over the chair and landing in a crazy position on the floor. I think it hurt, but I was too mortified to recognize that. I am not sure if it was a prank or not, but what an awful start.

I started out being very quiet, trying to absorb knowledge like a sponge. I questioned whether I was good enough. I wondered why they needed someone right out of school when the rest of them were so far along in their successes already. Was I going to be helpful in any way whatsoever?

Ultimately, the two years I spent there turned out to be incredible. I learned so much about all areas of the bank, rather than being in one. I was around the best minds and hopefully contributed somewhat as my confidence grew. This first job was the most satisfying of any I had in the field.

"I started out being very quiet, trying to absorb knowledge like a sponge. I questioned whether I was good enough."

Photo during early work years

BANKING AND INVESTMENT BANKING
FOR NINETEEN YEARS!

I t is hard to believe I lasted nineteen years in the financial world. I loved the challenge of it, but it was not satisfying in virtually any way. The hours were terrible—often seven a.m. until late at night, over and over. The stress with deadlines was omnipresent. Many coworkers seemingly had a knife ready to stick in your back at the slightest chance because the goal was to get promoted and to move up the ladder.

Over the course of that time, I worked for Chemical Bank, then Goldman Sachs, then Morgan Stanley (then a brief stint at ICM), and finally back to Chemical Bank. These were all highly respected financial institutions. Chemical was the predecessor bank prior to mergers with Manufacturers Hanover, JP Morgan Chase, and Bank One. At various times during the nineteen years across the different firms, I was a financial analyst, head of an internal planning group, investment banker doing mergers and corporate financings, head of a management analysis group, and ultimately senior vice-president and Chief of Staff to the president of Chemical Bank worldwide. I was also a member of the executive committee of the bank.

Probably the biggest challenge in the last role was to oversee the merger of Chemical with Mannie Hannie, as it was called. It was technically very complicated to send out bank-wide instructions to calculate merger cost savings, to integrate overlapping departments, and to track it all in real time. Worse was the massive politics involved with everyone trying to protect their turf and be the chosen one between two banks to stay. Interestingly enough, I was chief of staff for the prior chairman of Manufacturers Hanover in my role, who was named president of Chemical Bank after the merger, while the chairman of Chemical Bank (who I knew well) was chairman of the new entity.

I was not going to change who I was as a person in my management style. Despite the tough hours and demands, I always tried to create a team atmosphere where we supported and liked each other. It sometimes got me in trouble as I could be seen as one of the team rather than a distant enough manager or authority figure. But if I was spending that many hours with a group of people, I tried very hard to make it friendly. It already was an environment filled with stress, deadlines, exacting demands and long days.

I was still terrified of public speaking. My childhood days of being shushed and silenced, plus the parental expectations of my excelling, were firmly implanted in the rest of my life. I came up with very inventive reasons why someone else should give speeches rather than me. My biggest terror was being behind a podium in a huge auditorium. I felt as though everyone was judging me. Sitting around a table, even with forty people, was bad but much more manageable.

Ultimately, because I had to give weekly updates to the management committee of the bank, I became somewhat more comfortable. The chairman and president were really good people; once when my back went out from stress, they told me to give the presentation while lying flat on my back on the floor next to the table. It helped apparently that they suffered from chronic back pain themselves... a sympathetic audience.

Those ending Chemical Bank days had come a long way from my early Goldman Sachs days, but technologically were still in the dark ages. At Goldman, we used to walk into their management committee with life-size posters that we put on easels. I kid you not. They were heavy, and half the time they either fell off or the easel tipped over. I still have nightmares of those meetings, and the Goldman leadership were not nice people—quite the opposite at that time.

The secret at these financial institutions was to work very hard, to complete a consistently high-quality product, and to conform (dare

I say kiss ass?). It also helped to build allies higher up the corporate ladder who would look out for you. It always felt completely draining, and I never got over wondering both whether I belonged there and whether I was a fake, fooling them into thinking I was valuable. Most of all, it was not fulfilling.

The two investment banks in general had much more highly talented people than the commercial bank, but also were much more ruthless. Between the hours and the demands and the stress, I did have to have some outlets... They were just hard to fit in when I was so tired! My friends complained that I never spent time with them and that bothered me greatly.

Roommates in NYC on a field trip to DC

HOME LIFE IN THE CITY

Home was on the upper east side of Manhattan. The apartment was picked out by my two roommates who were classmates at business school, while I took a vacation in the first part of the summer. It was a nice three bedroom with a balcony and near an express bus to get to Wall Street.

One roommate was a huge Notre Dame fan and never stopped touting the Irish. At one point we hurled the Notre Dame fight song album off the balcony, thankfully not decapitating anyone on the street. The other roommate was a tall, athletic guy who grew up in Wisconsin and also loved sports. We all had jobs at banks.

We settled into a bachelor pad existence. None of us could cook to save our lives. Remember my mom's specialty was tuna noodle casserole... Our worst attempt was inviting people over for Thanksgiving dinner, and the damn turkey never cooked. Saturday morning ritual for one of the roommates, which I happily joined in, was cleaning the apartment in our underwear.

I started going to a Catholic church nearby and joined a young adult's group. The group had a lot of activities and evolved into some friends to hang out with and even a girl to date. Yes, I was still not admitting that I was more attracted to guys, or I was afraid to take that step where others would know.

"It was half gay and half straight, and no one cared either way."

TWO OTHER FREQUENT HANGOUTS

There was a great piano bar called Brandy's on the Upper East Side, which is still there decades later. They had different pianists and singing waiters every night. Guests were encouraged not only to make song requests, but to go up and sing songs with a mic. There were many late nights there with many drinks. It was half gay and half straight, and no one cared either way. I loved to listen to music, to sing, and to glance at handsome guys.

Across the street from my second Upper East Side apartment was a Mexican place called Tuba City. They had a Sunday brunch with unlimited strong and large blue Margaritas. We were often there from noon to 4:00, and then the day was essentially over as we collapsed.

I continued my habit of loving to be around friends but having a truly special one with whom I could confide anything (except my sexuality) and vice versa. There was one incredible friend in each of the early apartments which made life so much better.

I could tell my roommate about the co-workers that had knives out and the clients from anywhere, including Birmingham, Alabama, who took me to the all-white male club and regaled each meal with derogatory comments about women, non-Christians, gays, blacks—anyone who was not a white Christian male. It was truly awful because I could not in my corporate role lash out at a client, but I never laughed or joined in at all.

"I remember walking up and down the block as many as ten times to be sure absolutely no one was in eyesight and then dashing into the bar. It was pathetic."

SNEAKING OUT

I was going out on dates with a cute Irish Catholic girl from the young adults' group, but it was becoming increasingly clear that I preferred hanging out with my close male friends. Nothing ever happened with any of those friends physically; it really was just great bonding. But I needed to explore my physical yearnings for men and see if they were real and as strong as what was building up inside me.

So while dating the aforementioned cute Irish girl, I sneaked off to a bar about eight blocks away that was a gay bar. I remember walking up and down the block as many as ten times to be sure absolutely no one was in eyesight and then dashing into the bar. It was pathetic. But a whole new life was inside the bar—loud music that were the hits of the time, hot guys, amazing lights, adventure, secrets...

I didn't tell a soul about this, not even my best friend. But I was hooked. I am embarrassed to say that my first sex with a guy was in the bathroom of the bar. It was fast (as I recall very fast due to me) with a blond-haired, blue-eyed hunk named Jim. Since it was my first time with a guy, I was in love and planning marriage... not really, but you get the idea. To Jim, it was probably just one of many encounters for fun. I went back looking for Jim many times, and definitely there was the validation that boys excited me more than girls. I was twenty-nine when this first male/male experience happened. I never looked back after that.

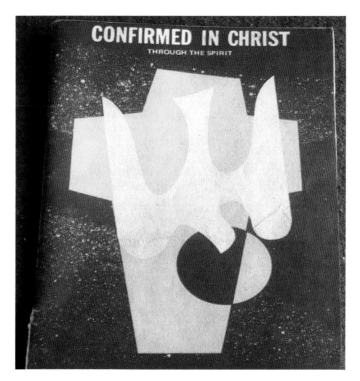

Confirmation

RELIGION—A TANGLED WEB

I decided after a few years of attending St Joseph's to ask the priest about being accepted into the Catholic church. This, as you remember, started with my going to mass in college. He said it involved personal and group instruction over a series of months. I said let's go ahead. The church represented a place where I could actively worship with others and pray about my personal dreams and goals. Leaving mass, I always felt inspired and that I was a kinder person. Some of their positions truly bothered me, but I chose to make it my personal worship rather than embracing policies counter to mine.

Later in life, I realized that a physical church was not necessary for my spiritual goals. At this time, the church served a very affirmative part of my life. I did know that this would bring up wounds from my parents' past, when their families did not support a Methodist marrying a Catholic. I had learned that neither side of the family supported their marriage nor attended the wedding. My dad was ex-communicated from the church for not signing a document saying they would raise us as Catholics. My mom was an outcast from my dad's family for years as a non-Catholic, although slowly, but not ever completely accepted.

And here I am reversing that painful decision. Nonetheless, I did go through with it, and I was received into the church by the bishop in a ceremony where one of my Denison friends flew out to be my sponsor. I took St Francis of Assisi as my patron saint because of his love of nature and animals and overall kindness.

My mother was *not* happy, while my father secretly sent me gifts in the mail. Meanwhile, my brother was about to marry a Jewish woman, and again neither side of the family in the generation before us was ecstatic, to say the least. I have always accepted everyone's personal religious choices and do not understand how most of our global wars and interpersonal battles have been fought over religious differences.

However, we did not discuss the subject of religion at home at all going forward.

It was somewhat ironic that I was accepted into the Catholic church and attending mass regularly, while at the same time I had discovered finally that I was gay. I was worshipping at a place that called me a sinner rather than loving all of God's creatures. I did feel at peace during mass but had the dichotomy of completely disagreeing with many of the church's policies.

Patron Saint

"we did not discuss the subject of religion at home at all going forward."

"But hearing them say they loved me and wanted me to be happy was what I needed to hear. I knew they would always be there."

COMING OUT

After I had become totally confident that I preferred men, I knew that I needed to tell my immediate family and my closest friends. This was not an easy task. I grew up in Ohio at a time where I had never even met an openly gay person and my family was loving, but conservative. Having no role models and knowing the same for my family, my biggest message to them was that I am exactly the same person they have always known. Being gay is one of one hundred parts that add up to Carl, and a label does not define me. I also had to assure them that it was not a choice—it was part of my nature, and I could not change that. God created us and loved all of us as beautiful creatures.

I knew that they had no clue, and that this would be a shock. I didn't want to spring it on them face to face or on a phone call where they had to give an immediate reaction. Also, since I have always been a better writer than speaker, I thought mailing them a letter saying exactly what I wanted to say was the way to go. They would have time to absorb it before our conversation then too. I can't tell you the number of hours I devoted to making that letter as direct and explanatory as possible.

An uncomfortable few days passed after which I suggested we speak. While they were not waving banners and joining PFLAG, they did say all they wanted for me was to be happy. But their concern was that it would be considerably more difficult being happy as a gay man. They clearly knew that not everyone would accept it, and that there were stereotypes and prejudices people in the Midwest definitely have. They asked me not to tell any relative outside our immediate family, which also implied they felt a degree of shame. That request was never broken (until now). They made it clear that they thought that my life would not be the same. They thought it might be a phase and a choice that I would reverse later. They suggested seeing a therapist. Does this sound like many movies you have watched?

But hearing them say they loved me and wanted me to be happy was what I needed to hear. I knew they would always be there.

Brothers

I AM AN UNCLE!

Our family became larger later on, and I happily became an uncle! I love little kids, and they were incredible to play with. It created a family scene which would not be available to me, it seemed. But the next best alternative!

At the same time, I have to say that upon my brother getting married, our personal relationship was never quite the same as when we were growing up. Part of that is inevitable. Part of it was unfortunate family dynamics that entered the picture. But I always value the times when we can have a one-on-one conversation.

Niece and nephews

Hamptons Houses and friend for golf

The Hamptons

The Pines

THE HAMPTONS AND FIRE ISLAND HOUSES

I needed an escape from the stress of banking and that happened with taking summer houses on Long Island with friends. There couldn't have been a bigger dichotomy between my experiences in the Hamptons versus Fire Island. In both cases, houses were rented for the summer with about eight friends. I *love* the beach, and summer is my favorite season. This was an escape from the steaming sidewalks of New York City.

The Hamptons houses I put together with friends from work. They were all straight, and we all knew each other really well. It was a time of barbecues, hanging by the pool, golf and summer drinks. Everyone had a blast, and we tried it in several different towns in the Hamptons—East Hampton, Westhampton and Quogue. The house had half guys and girls and was so relaxing. Never an argument… just loving our escape. The biggest issue we ever had was one pool turning pea green over the course of the summer—gross! Driving was necessary to get there and to go around to grocery stores or restaurants or just to window shop in the upscale towns.

Fire Island was almost all gay on the other hand. The beach in the Pines is renowned as one of the most beautiful in the world, and people came from all over the world to stay there. There were no cars; you took a ferry across the bay to get to the Pines. Once sitting on the upper deck of the ferry and crossing the water, you immediately felt like you were heading to a magical place. People walked on boardwalks everywhere, and houses were also spectacular, but mostly wood and built on sand and very different from the more traditional Hamptons.

The Pines could be very restful or very wild, depending on the house. My favorite part was hanging on the beach most of the day. There were traditions. The first, called low tea, had everyone gathering at a bar at 7:00 or so every night. Then you drifted to high tea at another bar around 8:30 or 9:00. They were packed with hot men, many in speedos. Dancing and flirting and heading to the beach to make out were abundant. Housemates headed back to their houses for late tremendous, cooked dinners at 10:30 or so, and then you had the option of going out until bars closed at four. When you fill a small island with gay men, anything goes. My life there was way more tranquil than most. I have never been a late-night bar person. But I have always been an early morning beach meditation fan. The quiet, the waves, the sun creeping up... total bliss!

I really liked both the Hamptons and The Pines in different ways. I was closer friends with my roommates in the Hamptons, and it was more relaxing. The Pines, on the other hand, had the excitement of not knowing when I might meet someone I was attracted to. But I still was not comfortable sometimes being part of a large gay enclave.

Playing golf with Bob Flicker in the Hamptons

Painting my face for Duke

MARCH MADNESS

March was always my favorite month of the year because college basketball was entering its tournament—March Madness! In my opinion, college basketball is the greatest sport to watch because they play so much harder than pros and have incredible home court support.

My two favorite teams are Ohio State and Duke. Ohio State is obvious. I loved Duke as a result of so many amazing players and Coach K being the best coach ever with a clean program.

I went to eight Final 4's, usually with three friends. They were unbelievably fun because the designated city would be packed by students from the four colleges. My first one was in Denver at a 20,000-seat arena where we were close to the action. We also went to visit the Air Force Academy. After that year, the NCAA switched to large, domed stadiums in places like Seattle, Indianapolis, New Orleans and Minneapolis where our lottery tickets were so high up the players looked like ants. These were real Bob Uecker seats!

But the fun was going to crowded bars, parks, rallies, and even painting our faces—I guess reliving college in a way. Duke lost to UNLV in 1990 in Denver, the ultimate bad guys versus the good guys. But they got revenge the following year and won the national championship, beating UNLV in the semifinal. Some say the 1992 tournament was the greatest ever played as Christian Laettner caught a long pass and made a shot as time expired against Kentucky in the regional final. Then Duke won over the Fab 5 of Michigan in the final.

"The group was comprised of the best and brightest, as everyone craved a job at Morgan Stanley."

MY EXPERIENCE WITH A FABRICATED SEXUAL HARASSMENT CLAIM

While at Morgan Stanley, I was head of an internal management consulting group that took on projects across the firm with the various divisions. The group was comprised of the best and brightest, as everyone craved a job at Morgan Stanley. We hired many analysts right from undergrad, associates from grad schools, and more experienced members with job experience. There was a hierarchical structure, but teams were usually composed of people at all three levels. The analysts were hand chosen and brilliant; many went on to have hugely successful careers.

At any time, we had up to fifty projects and my three direct reports, and I doled them out with my overall supervision. One female analyst from a very wealthy family was at the analyst level and was failing at her job, according to the managers above her. She somehow got wind that she was going to be fired by one of my direct reports, and incredibly she concocted a sixteen page, very detailed letter of how I had been sexually harassing her during her time there. It was so extensive and detailed that I would have believed it if I didn't know every word was a lie.

She sent it to the management committee, and suddenly, they had to investigate by interviewing everyone in my department. I could not tell them I was gay and had no interest in women because that would have also hurt my career at that time. I simply had to respond to each supposed incident and say that it never happened.

At the same time, I was having a consensual relationship with a guy who did not directly report to me but was at Morgan Stanley. It was my first real gay relationship, and I was head over heels. He was a first-year analyst, an athlete, second in his class, and very handsome. He initiated it all by inviting me over to dinner, which was unusual, and I didn't know what to do at first when his hand appeared on my knee. We had a passionate but tempestuous dating life, and I was worried first that they would believe the woman's fabrication and second that they would uncover my gay relationship. In that sense, the harassment claim from a woman was incredibly ironic, but at the time it was anything but humorous.

After the investigation, they told me they found no evidence of her claims and that everyone had backed me up. She left the company, but a friend in HR told me they paid her $50,000. It was an incredibly unsettled time, destroyed my ability to manage there, and taught me always to carefully look at both sides when a sexual harassment accusation is claimed. I do believe the overwhelming majority of sexual harassment claims have some or complete substance in truth, but my case proved not all of them. You can be put under the microscope for ulterior motives on the part of the supposed victim. I was incredibly angry but had to stay composed.

This event essentially ruined my previously good experience at Morgan Stanley; after all the upheaval, I had to transfer to an entirely new area of the bank, which I did not like at all. I also was thrust into projects where I had no prior experience and there was a set way to complete the tasks, e.g., mostly constructing prospectuses.

"I tried to stick it out for a while, but ultimately left the firm."

THE NEW YORK TIMES,
FRIDAY, JULY 3, 1981

A20   L

RARE CANCER SEEN
IN 41 HOMOSEXUALS

Outbreak Occurs Among Men
in New York and California
—8 Died Inside 2 Years

NYT article on beginning of AIDS crisis

HIV?? WHY ME?

I'm sure you have all either read books or have seen movies or plays about the very beginning of the AIDS crisis. People were dying very quickly from a mysterious illness that was particularly striking the gay community. While the movies and plays and books are quite strong and graphic, it is impossible to describe the fear going on around us. The worst part besides the rapid deterioration and death was that no one knew what caused it. How could it be transmitted? Through touch? Food? Kissing? Air? Why did it seem to be targeted at gay men? Suffering people became pariahs and were in some cases not accepted or treated at hospitals. But in fact, there *was* no treatment—people often died alone. Healthy people had a paranoia previously unforeseen but justified. No one knew before that there was such a thing as unsafe sex, much less that it could result in a terrible disease. I had no clue that any behavior in my past was not safe, extremely limited as it was with males.

When the very first diagnostic tests came out for the virus, I went in for a test. I was not nervous because I had only come out fairly recently and had one relationship, plus very few casual encounters. My doctor called me in days later for the results and said I was positive. A flood of emotions went through me. First of all, it seemed to be a death sentence. Second, I felt unbelievably unlucky given my extremely limited experiences with guys. Third, I had to take care of myself and be strong, but also prepare everything in case I passed away shortly.

It was difficult to focus on anything but this. While I continued working, I essentially hibernated for about three months, pretty much in shock. I wrote a will and other essential documents, canceled many upcoming plans, and worked on getting my mindset to a position of taking care of myself and being as healthy as I possibly could be. I felt terrible for my friends who were suffering.

It was hard to overlook the fact that no one knew they were doing anything potentially harmful prior to this mysterious disease. In addition,

I knew many people who had been very promiscuous and somehow were not positive. While being happy for them, I felt unbelievably unlucky given the unfortunate timing of my finally coming out and my very few dabblings at gay sex. As a result, overriding all this was: *WHY ME?*

ary Miller, the musical director, conducting the New York Gay Men's Chorus.

Music: Gay Men's Chorus and Gues

By JOHN ROCKWELL

HE 1980's have seen a quite remarkable proliferation of homosexual choruses; later this week the Gay and Lesbian Association of Choruses will hold second triannual convention, this in Minneapolis, and more than members are expected. Monday

in 1876 as part of the effort to raise money in France to build the Statue of Liberty.

The cantata is only five minutes long and is hardly of major musical importance — it is rather like Gounod's "Wellington's Victory." But the timeliness was nice, and the sight of the combined choruses, the lovely Tully Hall organ and the gleaming instrumental ensemble was spectacular.

when the two groups combine results were not so focused a pressive as when the New sang alone.

Both choruses also sho smaller units drawn from ranks. There were Seattle's dros Singers and the New Y Gay Men's Chorus Chambe both serious chamber ensem the Emerald City Volunteer to campy Broadway reperto

The New York City Gay Men's Chorus

AFTERSHOCKS OF MY DIAGNOSIS

It took me several months to wrap my head around this development. Most of that time, I was honestly getting ready for the worst. There was no known medication, and it felt like I was just in a waiting game for an opportunistic infection to strike. Every cold or upset stomach or infection was worrisome that it might mean more. Many people around me were getting sick and dying incredibly quickly.

My first reaction was to withdraw from everything. The news felt like a death sentence. As I said, I prepared a will and got my papers in order. I canceled tons of activities including a summer house rental. I was basically resigned that I had little time left.

But slowly I realized that life was going on and withdrawing from it would be the worst thing I could do. I broke the news to my parents and brother, who were devastated but gave upbeat messages to fight and believe the best.

I decided later to join the New York City Gay Men's Chorus, once I emerged from my self-imposed cocoon, both for a singing outlet, but more importantly for a group of men confronting the same situation. The chorus sang concerts at Carnegie Hall and Avery Fisher Hall, and they were high quality. Putting 100-200 gay men together would always have drama, but it also produced a community caring for each other and created some new close friendships.

While that was the benefit of the chorus, the downside was that it was being hurt severely by deaths in its ranks. We sang at so many memorial services with inspirational songs and dedications, but the deaths were a reminder of the precariousness of my situation too. Over 200 chorus members ultimately succumbed to AIDS.

A decade went by, and so far, I was hanging in there. Having the virus meant getting regular blood tests to see the level of your T cells, your immune helpers. Mine were dropping every year.

"The mayor of NYC, Ed Koch, and President Reagan essentially ignored AIDS."

AN INCREDIBLE LOSS OF FRIENDS AND T CELLS

It was a very frightening time to be living in NYC, one of the epicenters getting ravaged by deaths. Most of the people dying were young, creative people who were taken *way* too early. The talent drains from theater, music, film, fashion, dance, etc. were devastating. Just the theater industry alone lost so many amazing stars and "stars-to-be."

I saw many friends still attempting to live a semi-normal life who were increasingly gaunt or who had the telltale marks of Kaposi's sarcoma. They would be here one day and gone the next.

Meanwhile the papers were mentioning this, but not in a widespread manner. The mayor of NYC, Ed Koch, and President Reagan essentially ignored AIDS. The gay community was hit hardest and marginalized even further than ever. Sick people were treated as pariahs.

I lost many people very dear to me. It was also hard to avoid the reality that my immune system was getting worse continuously. The long hours of work at the bank and the stress of deadlines were certainly contributing. I began to wonder what I should do to preserve life as long as possible.

My T cells reached the "dangerous" level of 200 in the early 90s, which was the clinical definition of having AIDS. At that point, only one medication was on the market that had shown any positive benefit in some portion of patients. It was called AZT, and an equal number of doctors and patients also thought it caused more damage than benefit. It was labeled as poison in some prominent NYC gay publications.

With no other choice, I tried AZT. Like many other people, it made me constantly nauseated and with terrible upset stomachs. I simply could not tolerate that quality of living and gave up the experiment. It seemed like an "all is lost" time.

The famous lighthouse at Hilton Head, South Carolina

It was a tough course, and we were struggling, but nothing matched the 18th hole. My brother was suddenly dribbling the ball not very far in consecutive swings. He got pissed and stopped. My friend had an incredible slice on his tee shot, and his ball was ricocheting across multiple balconies of condos to the right of the course. I was doing okay until I had a short wedge shot to the green, which I skulled and hit way over the green and halfway across the pond in front of the lighthouse.

We gave up, laughing at how awful we were. But the nineteenth hole made up for it, and it was an incredible catch-up time reminiscing on Denison and the fraternity brothers.

A FEW DANGLING PARTICIPLES

Meanwhile, life continued in my nineteen years in the financial field, amazingly enough. My brother was also working very hard as a lawyer after attending Princeton's Woodrow Wilson School of Public and International Affairs and Columbia for his law degree. I was really proud of him.

I was realizing that my life had to change out of business to satisfy my creative side, and I have always believed my brother wanted to be in government policy rather than corporate law. He was married and had a smaller circle of friends—mostly sticking to home life. I was not married and gave a lot more precedence to my friendships, which were and are incredibly important to me.

We did try to gather our closest Denison friends when possible. For example, we took a golf vacation at Hilton Head and played the famous course with the lighthouse on the 18th hole.

Mom and Dad had also settled into a pattern of his work, family get-togethers, and sales trips. They both drank more in the later stages of their lives, but Dad handled it better. Mom always had to have two martinis before we ordered dinner, and we used every power in our book to not let her order a third on an empty stomach. She was the giver of the family, taking care of so many people, but after too many martinis Chuck and I often would hear her say we ruined her life—me by being gay and Chuck by his choice of wife. It was hard to hear, but then the next morning she would be back to Mom. Just a big sigh.

Dad

Within a half hour he had passed. I truly believe he was waiting for me to get there to say goodbye and to help Mom immediately in her grief. I often picture that half hour as a minor miracle during a time of grief.

Dad was a role model for honesty, ethics, doing the right thing, and working hard while also having time for fun.

LOSING MY DAD

Leukemia ran on my dad's side of the family, and he was diagnosed with it also. Dad had always been a very strong person, never complaining about any aches or pains, always stoic. Classic German.

He remained that way through several years of deteriorating. He became weak and lost a lot of weight. Every time he even slightly bumped into something; it created a huge purple bruise. There was no treatment that was going to prevent the inevitable, but he was the same person to the end. He still had a joke on command.

I had always been closer to my mom and had not had the same insights into my dad. The illness changed that. Suddenly, we were talking about so many very personal things, and his wisdom and kindness and generosity of spirit were flowing out. Dad loved being the life of the party but at the same time was insecure and desperately wanted to be liked. He also was very smart and felt underappreciated at the company where he had worked for over forty years. I grew to understand him in a way I never had and realized I also shared the strong desire to be accepted. He was such a giving person to his extended family and everyone around him. He did have emotions that were seldom expressed but emerged now. There are some blessings with illnesses that linger, as long as there is no major pain involved. It is odd to say so, but I felt blessed to have this personal time with my dad as he became weaker and weaker.

I was working one morning, and my mom called to say I had better get home as soon as possible, as Dad was on his last legs. My work cohorts were amazing and leaped into action with getting me car service and the first flight and helping me pack. I arrived and took a cab directly to the hospital. Mom was sitting by his bed, and I held Dad's hand and told him how incredible a father he always was.

"I now officially had AIDS"

1995: A YEAR THAT CHANGED MY LIFE

I was continuing to work and was back at Chemical Bank for a second go around. April rolled around, and four of us flew to Seattle for the March Madness Final 4. It was the usual weekend of drinking too much, enjoying the games, and staying up late.

After coming back to NYC, I felt very weak and tired and feverish. I could not even get out of bed. My doctor sent me to the hospital, and they determined I had pneumocystis, a bacterial pneumonia that was an opportunistic infection from AIDS. My T cells were also down to 60, when normal levels are 800-2000.

It was a touch and go situation in the hospital for quite a while. I had IVs everywhere it seemed. However, with prayer and the support of my friends and a lot of rest, I pulled through. They sent me home, still on an IV for more months with a home nurse. I had lost a lot of weight and was very weak.

I now officially had AIDS, rather than just being HIV+. The definition of AIDS at the time was having an opportunistic infection related to the HIV virus and/or T cells under 200. I fit both definitions. It turned out to be the last day I worked in financial services. Working there for so long had obviously contributed to my tiredness and stress and overall health. If I had continued any longer in that environment, I would not be here today. I felt very lucky to be alive, and, fortunately, late 1995 was also the year protease inhibitors came out as the first effective treatment for AIDS. At the end of 1995, I started on a drug called Saquinavir. My treatment would have continual changes over the years as my doctor and I tried to determine what medicines were most effective in restoring my T cells to a less urgent crisis. Now, what next? Would this be an isolated incident or the beginning of many health emergencies? What would my day-to-day life be now? Was my life now irreparably changed? What would I have to look forward to?

ACT THREE
PUTTING IT TOGETHER

F rom *Sunday in the Park with George*

"Bit by bit
Putting it together
Piece by piece
Only way to make a piece of art
Every moment makes a contribution
Every little detail plays a part
Having just a vision's no solution
Everything depends on execution
Putting it together
That's what counts."

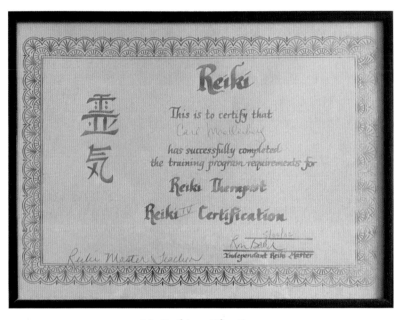

My Reiki certification

LEARNING ALTERNATIVE HEALING

When I felt up to it, I decided to study various healing modalities, both to use them on myself and to help others. This was a multi-year and multi-faceted study.

First, I took classes in Swedish technique and Shiatsu. I had always loved receiving massage and found that giving therapeutic touch to others left me very grounded. With soft music, candles, a table, and my new skills, I became completely focused on the person receiving my healing. While helping others, I was also helping myself stay grounded and in the moment. I also was a frequent receiver of massages.

Second, I studied Reiki for two years and became certified as a Reiki Master. Reiki is a form of alternative medicine called energy healing. Reiki practitioners use a technique called *palm healing* or *hands-on healing* through which a "universal energy" or life force called chi is transferred through the palms of the practitioner to the patient in order to encourage emotional or physical healing. Everything in life is, at its core, energy, and learning about energy transfer was an enlightening process.

Besides using it as a healing modality on many friends with AIDS or cancer, I also became very tuned in immediately to the energy of anyone in my presence. Over the years, this was invaluable in realizing who would be a valuable new friend or business colleague and who should be avoided at all costs.

Third, I took a six-month course with a Shaman who previously had teachers in Peru. This study was much more all-encompassing—embracing nature, discovering my spirit animal (a wolf), calling in spirit guides, drumming, joining fire ceremonies, and many others. I have to say that in the sessions where he worked on me as a healer for an hour, I left completely loving, open, and cleared out of negative thoughts.

All the classes (bodywork, Reiki, energy, etc.) allowed me to do volunteer work and give back to the community. Examples were manning the suicide hotline at the Trevor Project, being a counselor at a walk-in center called Identity House, becoming a life coach, and helping people with stress and pain issues with their bodies. It helped me put my energies into others.

WHEN VOLUNTEER WORK STRIKES CLOSE TO HOME

The Trevor Project, in particular, is an incredible organization. It is the world's largest suicide prevention and crisis intervention organization for LGBTQ youth in need.

The training is extensive because volunteers are literally on the line in potentially life-threatening situations. More often, the youth calling in are feeling isolated, alone, abandoned, sometimes thrown out of their homes and urgently require support and information. Volunteers work in pre-designated shifts fielding calls to the hotline.

Listening to the voices and often the tears of individuals who feel desperate and who express no hope is absolutely heartbreaking. First of all, we would make sure that they felt truly heard by someone who cared and wanted to help. Second, we would do our best to assess the seriousness and immediacy of the situation and in some cases to call for outside urgent intervention. Then we would work to keep them engaged in a real conversation to gather as much information as we could about where they are, their family members or friends, their home, and so forth. The more information we had, the more ideas we could suggest for organizations, groups and activities near them, in addition to asking them to rely on someone they trust within their lives.

I think what horrified me the most were the stories of children thrown out of their homes for being gay– for expressing how they were born and wanting to live their authentic lives. What parent could do that to their child? But it happens very often. I compare it to my conservative Midwestern parents who still expressed love and wanted the best for me.

I will never forget those plaintive voices. After ending each call, I had a deep yearning to be able to do more.

My ordination certificate

THE NEWLY ORDAINED MINISTER'S
WALK WITH A GOLDEN BIRD

I joined one other healing school, which also was focused primarily on energy and how to channel it for beneficial purposes. The teacher was well known and well written. The classes had free flowing dialogue and practitioner work. They were very spiritual, but not connected to a particular church as opposed to a Supreme Being.

The graduation ceremony after classes were completed allowed each of us to be ordained as a Minister in the Universal Church. It was a bright spring Sunday morning when the ordination took place. I left the ordination space in Midtown and decided to walk home about twenty-five blocks on such a gorgeous day. I turned onto Fifth Avenue and suddenly noticed a golden bird that I would never imagine would be in NYC. It seemed to belong in the Caribbean or some other tropical climate. I had certainly never seen a bird like this on a NYC sidewalk.

The bird proceeded to fly/walk with me for twenty-five blocks down Fifth Avenue. It would look at me, walk a bit with me, fly ahead, turn around and look at me to catch up. What was this???? Several other people on the street were excitedly exclaiming about and pointing at this unusual bird, but they did not know the bird was personally escorting me home! I was completely astonished.

I began talking to the bird about ten blocks along the walk. Thankfully I was not committed to Bellevue…. When we got to 25th Street, I told the bird I had to turn west to get home. The golden bird sat there and looked at me for perhaps thirty seconds. Then it flew right at me, grazing my hair and flew away.

I knew that something extraordinary had just occurred. When I reached home, I called my teacher to tell him about it. He seemed less surprised than I was and said it was clearly a sign that I was to use whatever gifts I had to serve the greater good.

Nothing like this ever happened again, but it is etched in my memory and resurfaces at important times. Sometimes we need to look carefully for signs, and other times they are magnificently displayed right in front of us.

MY SPIRITUALITY

I had previously gone through a discovery process of finding no spiritual value in the Methodist church and converting to Catholicism once I moved to New York City. I loved the sense of community and worshiping with a body of people who were sincere in their faith and in their desire to be better people. I honestly also loved the whole celebration and ritual of the mass. Going to church gave me a weekly place to go where I knew I would focus on God and "put myself in God's hands." It was comforting in rough times.

However, as time went on, it became far more difficult to embrace many of the policies of the Catholic church that are so counter to my beliefs.

Gays are not sinners. God loves all His creations. Women certainly deserve control over decisions affecting their bodies. The Pope is not infallible. Those are just a few examples of doctrine I do not share.

As a result, my faith did not diminish, but I chose to express it in my own spirituality, which did not require a church setting. Prayers and affirmations can be made at any moment of any day and in any setting. The Lord's Prayer means the same wherever it is recited. "Do unto others as you would have them do unto you" is a fabric of my daily life. Show kindness and respect and understanding for those around you day by day.

I still attended mass on occasion, but more importantly I formed my own concept of living spiritually, with both personal affirmations and actions toward others demonstrating my affirmations. Everyone will have times where they are disappointed in their actions, as I have on many occasions, but it is important to learn from them and to forgive yourself and others.

The Sydney Opera House. Sydney Australia

TRAVELING AROUND THE WORLD AFTER
A LONG RECOVERY

For nineteen years in the financial field, I had been working very long hours with relatively short vacations, which I normally used to lie on a beach and relax. When I developed full blown AIDS, I knew it was partially from the stress and long hours.

After a significant period of down time, during which I rested and then engaged in healing studies, I decided to embark with a straight friend on longer trips to places I had always wanted to experience. I paid for my friend to join me on these experiences, both for the company and for the security should I fall ill in a foreign country.

Over the course of a two-year period, we saw several incredible countries. My favorite was a trip that involved Los Angeles, Hawaii, Australia, and New Zealand. We broke up the very long flights with stays in L.A. and Hawaii. I absolutely loved Australia! The people were incredibly friendly and very outdoorsy. They were fun loving and welcoming. We traveled down the east coast from Sydney to Melbourne. It was January, which was summer there, and a huge blizzard occurred in NYC while I was gone. I couldn't resist sending my friends back home a picture from Bondi Beach, which was our first day in Sydney. Cheeky! The opera house and blue water were as spectacular as I had imagined.

In New Zealand we participated in a Māori tribe feast and dance. Of course, we were pulled from the audience to do the fierce shouting and facial expressions and threatening movements with them. I am sure I looked completely ridiculous! We also saw three different islands in Hawaii, which are breathtaking from the ground and from a helicopter.

There were so many other trips too! We would come home in between and then plan the next one. They included U.S. national

Māori Tribal Warrior Dance. New Zealand

The Parthenon Athens, Greece

parks, New Orleans, Paris and the French countryside, Greece and Turkey, Montreal, Italy, Cancun, London, and other shorter trips to beaches.

Some highlights among many: driving out of Paris through the chateau area. Each palace was extravagant and stunning. Everyone always says the French hate Americans, but that could not have been further from the truth for us. We got lost when we re-entered Paris from the countryside. So, we stopped to ask a Parisian for directions. He actually got into our car and directed us all the way to our hotel, even though it was completely out of his way. This was not my first trip to Paris, but I could go there over and over and love it more each time.

We flew to Athens on the Greece/Turkey trip to see the archeological sites. Then we took a ferry to Mykonos where everything was white buildings with blue trim and the brilliant blue sea. A paradise! A two-day excursion to Istanbul was eye-opening for the mosques and observing a different culture. You also could not walk half a block without someone wanting you to look at their carpets over tea.

I also realized what an incredibly young country America is after seeing so many structures that were centuries old. But America is beautiful and has such a wide range of unique landscapes, from the Grand Canyon to Yosemite to the Great Lakes to the Pacific Coast Highway—on and on. My parents had taken us on summer driving trips to most of the states in the country, so going overseas was the discovery part of the two years. I always came back tired but exhilarated by their history and traditions. I felt energized to be able to see many parts of the world that I never had the chance to see before.

Mexico

Tulum

Banks of the Loire River.
Divine Presence.

TALKING WITH GOD

The year is 1997, and I was sitting on the banks of the Loire River in France. It was mid-morning, and the sun was warm, but the breeze was fresh and cool. I was meditating all by myself in this unbelievably beautiful and tranquil location.

The previous few years had been the biggest challenge of my life. In 1995, I survived a very bad opportunistic infection (pneumocystis) after a lengthy stay in the hospital and then months of home IV therapy and home nurse care. I felt very fortunate to be alive and was now taking advantage of being able to travel to spectacular locations around the world.

As I looked out over the river, the sun in a clear blue sky was shining down on the river. It created a glistening, sparkling effect immediately above the river. The streaks or bolts of reflecting sunlight were then coming toward me almost mystically or supernaturally. Rowers were passing by smoothly on a completely quiet day except for the many birds.

I had no idea at that time what I was going to do with my life. It was a blank slate, and I had not painted on it yet. I was simply thrilled to be in this moment. Little did I know it was about to become the most meaningful event spiritually that I would ever experience.

Suddenly I heard a deep male voice in my head, as strong as if the person were sitting two feet away. I realized after a few moments that it was God speaking directly to me. The conversation went on for over fifteen minutes of amazement and bliss, after which I ran to my hotel to write in my diary the entire message. I wrote many pages incredibly rapidly so as not to forget anything said. I also took the picture you see here to memorialize the day, although it cannot do justice to the brightness of the river and sun sparks.

The summary of what God told me was that I should not give up. I was destined, despite all odds, to have a long life ahead of me. In that life, I would be loved and supported by many friends, and I would love and give back to them equally. God told me that I was to use that long life to create more beauty in the world. I was here for a reason. I was told that the reason would come to me, and it was in the arts. I contemplated what path I could take to create more beauty and joy for others, and images of theater appeared to me. It was then that I decided when I returned home that I would pursue a path to learning to help bring beauty through theater to audiences.

Fast forward twenty-five years. That decision has made me happier than ever. I hope that my part in the theater world has brought some happiness, thoughtfulness and joy to others. That day on the banks of the Loire was probably the most momentous and illuminating and unbelievable day in my life. I have no doubt it was a conversation with God and that I was steered to a completely new life that brought me joy and renewed my passion.

I have always sensed a divine presence does exist around us if we choose to be sensitive to listening for it. Sometimes it is extremely strong, such as a golden bird or a voice while in nature.

Other times it is in breezes or simply asking for the presence to give a sign that it is with me. I see the sign in many unique forms.

"God told me that I was to use that long life to create more beauty in the world."

At the Tony Awards

DISCOVERING MY NEW HOME ON BROADWAY

I would not be here today if I had gone back to investment banking, the long hours, and the stress. My conversation with God and my illness turned out to be a blessing as I completely changed my path. I decided to pursue producing on Broadway as my corridor to happiness in day-to-day life. I thought doing this on a part-time basis (almost as a hobby) would be a motivator to push on, to have new goals and something for which to live. It would be amazing to help create stories that have an impact on others. I would edge my way into this to create a meaningful life ahead.

However, one cannot suddenly raise their hand and say they are a Broadway producer. You actually need to know what you are doing! (Although sadly since then I have discovered many producers who have absolutely no clue.)

First, I signed up for some weekend intensive workshops on theater production put on by the Commercial Theater Institute. Then I was accepted into a fourteen-week program along with about twenty-five other aspiring producers. It delved into all aspects from the creative process to legal to marketing to fundraising to union rules, etc. There was always a prominent guest lecturer followed by open-ended questions from us. It was a terrific opportunity to learn some basics plus to network among people who might be partners later and to meet lead producers who would be valuable resources.

You cannot learn theater production by reading books or by talking, however. You can be much more knowledgeable, but the real learning is on the job. I would discover that as I threw myself into productions; each show would have its unique challenges in how to identify the demographic audience, to reach them by advertising/print/TV/social media, spirited discussions about the script, and a myriad of issues particular to the show—cast, set, costumes, sound, orchestrations, etc.

It was time to take a stab at theater producing, but little did I know how immersed I would become.

My first Tony Award
(for Spring Awakening)

INITIAL FORAYS and MY FIRST TONY AWARD

As a new producer, the biggest hurdle is to be accepted onto productions and to demonstrate that you are reliable, have good business advice and creative ideas, are a team player, and can raise the committed money. Without a track record, you must establish one, have your resume built, and your favorable reputation spread. The theater world is actually very small. A relatively small number of producers are putting on all the shows in a limited number of theaters. Everyone knows everyone.

I had a very fortuitous beginning. My very first investment (I wish it had been larger) was in *Wicked*, which of course turned out to be a huge hit and is still running. Once you invest in Broadway, you also have the right to invest in all the forthcoming productions of the show, such as national tours or in other countries. My very first investment has been the highest percentage return I have achieved over the eighteen years that have followed.

My first show where I was accepted as a co-producer was *Spring Awakening*. I had seen the show and was mesmerized by it at an off-Broadway house. The music by Duncan Sheik was haunting and gorgeous. The cast included three people who went on to become big stars—Jonathan Groff, Lea Michele, and John Gallagher, Jr. They were at the beginning of their careers, but they were clearly brilliant already.

The show was considered a risk because it dealt with many dark topics: suicide, abortion, first sexual experience, rebellion, and more. However, the combination of the cast, the best lighting I have ever seen (by Kevin Adams), and incredible direction by Michael Mayer made it a must see. We had groupies who had seen it over 100 times, as I discovered sitting among them as they cried and screamed on the closing night.

Spring Awakening won the Tony Award for Best Musical, and I was hooked on my new path. I could not have been more fortunate with my first investment and first producing picks. I also learned how it really does take a village to mount a show successfully—from the cast, the producing team, the band, the director and choreographer, the general manager, the stage manager, the dressers, the crew, the house management, the creatives for costumes, lighting, and set, obviously the writers—well, you get the idea. When we first gather to begin rehearsals, it is called a meet and greet, and everyone involved in the show fills a large room. Everyone has high hopes, and, in this case, they came true.

Wicked

Spring Awakening

The Tony Cabinet

BROADWAY IS DEFINITELY NOT JUST A HOBBY

When I started doing Broadway, I viewed it as a way to stay active, to use my creative side, and to find joy in the shows for which I was part of the producing team. I viewed it as a lifeline for me and better yet, it was not taxing to my health. I anticipated doing perhaps one show a year to keep the juices flowing and to have something to be excited about always on the horizon. Most importantly, I wanted to help tell stories that transformed audience members in some important way—identifying with situations in their own families, looking at issues in an entirely different way, becoming emotional at breathtakingly beautiful music.... At that time, I was not a lead producer, so it was not time consuming or draining at all. I could be a co-producer without major activity, which would drain my health. I started a website called BroadwayInvesting.com to educate others on what it entails to be involved with a show.

Apparently, I was still a person that could not do something in a small way, but rather I always threw myself wholeheartedly into the pursuit. In the sixteen years since *Spring Awakening* opened, I have been part of the producing team on about seventy shows across Broadway, London, Australia, and national tours. Making the leap from investment banking to theater was the best decision of my life. It has filled me with passion and delivered many moments of goosebumps or happy tears. I particularly love doing musicals (rock musicals especially), given my music background. This joy and passion has been the major reason I am still on this Earth.

It is incredible watching audiences be moved by the music or the story. That is the primary factor I look for in choosing new shows: Is there a message or a score that will profoundly affect the audience? While I do theater not as an occupation, but as a joy, about 2/3 of all the shows I either produced or invested in have made a profit, compared to the industry wide statistic of about twenty-five percent of shows making money. I look to find what will move people emotionally or intellectually and cause them to tell others that they *have* to see the show or the cast.

A nice recognition has also come from being involved with so many brilliant writers, directors, and cast members. I have been fortunate to now have 12 Tony Award statues as a producer in my glass display case. The 13th statue is on the way for Company! That makes me so happy and proud while recognizing that the whole village shares in those rewards.

MY PERSONAL CONNECTION WITH EACH SHOW

Each of those thirteen shows which garnered Tony Awards meant a lot to so many people, but I'd like to take a moment to say what was special about them individually to me. There were many elements of each that were truly special, so I am citing only the most important to me in choosing to be a part of the producing team. These are not in any particular order except I have to put *Hair* first, and I previously spoke about *Spring Awakening*.

Hair

- *Hair* The musical was first on Broadway in 1968 and was a statement of the times about peace, freedom, the anti-war movement, hippie counterculture and open love. The music has become beloved over the years. This is my favorite show of all I have ever done because the cast and everyone connected to the show reflected those values of peace and love and a free spirit. Never have I witnessed such a close bond across what we called the Tribe, both onstage and off, as in our 2009 revival. I truly loved everything about this run, and it will always have that special place in my heart.

Death of a Salesman

- ***Death of a Salesman*** Having the chance to work with Philip Seymour Hoffman about a year before his tragic passing is unforgettable.

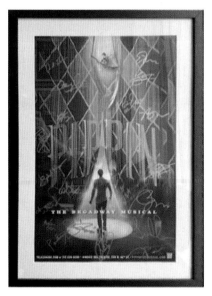

Pippin

- *Pippin* When doing a revival, I believe there needs to be a re-imagining of the show, a reason to bring it back. Diane Paulus putting *Pippin* under a circus roof with gymnastic performers was a brilliant backdrop to the wonderful Stephen Schwartz score.

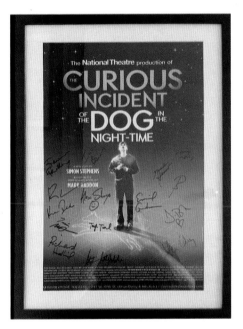

The Curious Incident of the Dog in the Night-Time

- *The Curious Incident of the Dog in The Night-Time* The National Theater of London is unparalleled in its productions of plays and their efforts for this show were amazing. The special visual effects of a boy on the autism spectrum seeming initially to be in a black box brought out the message of the story in a thrilling manner. This is an example of a play that had to be seen for its intellectual *and* emotional content. Any parent who has a child on the spectrum could deeply identify with the boy and his father.

War Horse

- ***War Horse*** This was another National Theater production which featured life-size horse puppets, each handled on stage by four trainers to make you believe you are observing real horses. When a horse made its first appearance, there was always a huge gasp. Soon into the show, the horses became real characters and not man-made creations.

Dear Evan Hansen

- ***Dear Evan Hansen*** Ben Platt. No more words needed. Just Kleenex.

Oklahoma

- *Oklahoma* This production was a revolutionary and dark portrayal of an American classic. I had mixed emotions about certain aspects of the production.

All the Way

- *All The Way* Bryan Cranston as LBJ was so convincing in the role of an important and controversial American President. He simply is a brilliant actor.

Angels in America

- ***Angels in America*** The re-telling of a devastating story that was important for a new generation of viewers to witness.

The Band's Visit

- ***The Band's Visit*** A chance and welcoming meeting of Israelis and Arabs occurring because of a lost Israeli band in powder blue dress uniforms. A true cultural unity message.

Hadestown

- **HADESTOWN** Every production element of the show was a master-piece by every part of the creative team.

- **COMPANY** Director Marianne Elliott had an idea to change the gen-der of the lead actor Bobby to a female. She had many conversations with Stephen Sondheim about not only that but many other new imag-inings for the show. He was very enthusiastic and made it to rehearsals and previews prior to passing away before the opening.

Chronology

Show	Role	Award	Year
Company	Producer	Best Revival of a Musical	2022
Hadestown	Producer	Best Musical	2019
Oklahoma!	Producer	Best Revival of a Musical	2019
Angels In America	Producer	Best Revival of a Play	2018
The Band's Visit	Producer	Best Musical	2018
Dear Evan Hansen	Producer	Best Musical	2017
The Curious Incident of The Dog In The Night	Producer	Best Play	2015
All The Way	Producer	Best Play	2014
Pippin	Producer	Best Revival of a Musical	2013
Death Of A Salesman	Producer	Best Revival of a Play	2012
War Horse	Producer	Best Play	2011
Hair	Producer	Best Revival of a Musical	2009
Spring Awakening	Producer	Best Musical	2007

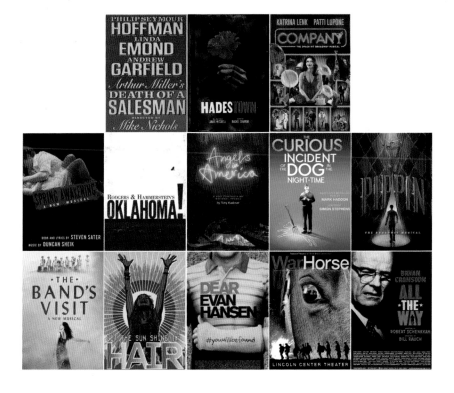

My entourage with Michael Forsyth at the far left.

With Bobby Sain

MY ENTOURAGE FOR BROADWAY OPENING NIGHTS

Opening night of a show is a big deal! It is the culmination of a lot of hard work, often over years. It is the presentation of the show for everyone that had a piece in making it come to life, plus celebrities. It is a packed cheering house to an appreciative cast.

Opening night also means that reviews will be coming out at around 10 p.m. after the show. The scene always has some tension until the reviews appear on our phones at the after parties. The mood then becomes either raucous fun or more somber, depending on what the critics (especially the NY Times) had to say.

There is a party nonetheless after the show, and everyone loves to dress up and be "in the room." Depending on my allotment of tickets, I would put together what I called my entourage to be there with me. They would be my close friends who loved theater and were always a very good-looking younger group. We had a blast! I cannot tell you how many "varied" comments I got whispered in my ear about the handsome guys especially. Little did they know that the majority of my closest friends are straight and there just to share in the excitement.

**With Anthony Del Negro
at the Tony Awards**

WHAT LESSONS DID I LEARN FROM BROADWAY?

The single most important one is that the story is everything. It needs to resonate with audiences in a deeply personal way. If the show is a musical, the lyrics need to advance the story, and the score must be unique and memorable.

I personally prefer more intimate shows, whether plays or musicals. I know that many tourists especially love huge song and dance numbers. I am looking instead for meaning or transformation from my two hours there from the interactions portrayed.

The second most important lesson was that who you partner with is crucial. As with every field, there are great collaborators versus bullies; there are ethical people versus those without a moral compass; there are producers with various reasons for being on Broadway, which may or may not align with yours (self-promoting personal fame versus creating art). There are some producers with a wealth of knowledge about every facet of producing and others with virtually none. The longer you are doing shows, you develop a personal list that has a YES column and a NO column for whether you would work with them again. I have had the opportunity to work with many brilliant leaders. When you collaborate with an amazing producer or director, you will run to their next project over and over.

Being successful on shows involves having a great creative sense along with a solid business understanding. A lot of producers have one or the other, but not both. I loved working with well-rounded partners, where we were speaking the same language.

Another important lesson, which might seem obvious, is that you need to figure out the demographic that will embrace your show and then determine how to reach them. Every show is different, and the campaign needs to be tailored to your specific show. I have to say I have seen marketing campaigns that seem to be very cookie cutter and similar across completely different subject matters. That usually is a recipe for disaster.

Lastly, it helps to have well-known, amazing star power. But if the show is good enough, a very talented, tight ensemble can light up the stage.

But the biggest lesson I learned is that:

I
LOVE

BROADWAY

"There are unfortunately many side effects of either having HIV for four decades, or the medicine, or both."

I AM A LONG-TERM SURVIVOR WITH MANY DEBILITATING CONSEQUENCES

No, I was not cast on Survivor. I would have only lasted two days. But I did become a part of managing the many difficult side effects of the HIV virus and medications as a long-term survivor.

In the early days, the goal before medical treatments was simply to take care of oneself to improve the chances of staying alive. It was unbelievably sad seeing so many friends succumb very rapidly. Starting in 1995, protease inhibitors became available as a significant way to manage the virus. After that, advances were made with multiple choices of drugs. My doctor and I went through many different variations of medicines and ultimately arrived at a "cocktail" of three that seemed to have the best impact. These were not Singapore Sling cocktails from college, but three drugs that I had to remember to take at the right time twice a day. Lapses could create big problems with the virus multiplying.

Ultimately, we arrived at the place where my viral load is undetectable, meaning that even at minute levels, HIV cannot be discovered in my blood. This also means that I cannot transmit the virus to others, although I am safe all the time anyway. Once I reached undetectable levels, I have never had one time where the viral load did become detectable again in a very long time. My immune helping T cells made it up to 400 to 600—not normal, but not threatening either.

There are unfortunately many side effects of either having HIV for four decades, or the medicine, or both. Chronic stomach problems are a major issue. My physical problems also include what is called lipodystrophy, which started around 2015. Lipodystrophy refers to a medical problem where there is an abnormal distribution of fat in the body. What results is that fat accumulates in the stomach area, and both muscle mass and fat are taken away from arms and legs. To date, there is only one injectable treatment, and it did not work on me.

As a result, my thirty-two-inch waist that I had for a long time was expanding rapidly due to a medical condition. I have always prided myself on being in good shape, and I now have a large stomach, which I cannot do anything about. I also could not explain it to others as I was hiding my HIV condition. It is a blow to my feeling good about myself.

More importantly, the mass in my stomach has adverse effects on the functioning of internal organs, causing very sharp pains with movement and affecting my breathing as well. When I turn my body to one side, I frequently get an incredibly sharp pain in my side, which causes me to keel over for a few minutes. I have to look straight ahead and not turn, or I am suddenly in bad pain. It has also led to my passing out suddenly at events, on the street, at home, etc.

Meanwhile, my legs, arms, knees, ankles, and wrists have gotten tinier and tinier. They are very susceptible to injury, which has occurred multiple times. Again, I train to try to build them up, but it is uncontrollable. The loss of mass also contributed to my having to have foot surgery, which has not resulted in any improvement two years later. It has gotten hard to walk very far between my hurting foot, weak ankles, knee pain, my hips locking, and movement of my body resulting in dizziness or the sharp side pains.

I realize people live through *much* more severe problems than this. But I wanted to include this because some people now take HIV casually since it is presumably manageable. However, it has severely affected the quality of my life and my ability to be the active person I once was. It has also caused me to be very down at times due to my many limitations and pains. I have always been an active and an optimistic person, but those traits have been put to the test. I have not told many people about the depression my condition has caused, but it has been major and has led to greater isolation. Being alone much more often and very immobile is debilitating.

"It has severely affected the quality of my life and my ability to be the active person I once was."

"I am particularly nervous about this chapter."

LEARNING TO DEAL WITH ANXIETY

Long term survivors also frequently encounter severe anxiety. Mine has been getting worse with each passing year. Very often an event involving going out causes anxiety resulting in an upset stomach, nausea, vertigo, lightheadedness, etc. That becomes severe if it involves an important meeting or a large group of people.

But now it has extended sometimes to even a simple activity such as lunch or an errand. The effects are less severe but nonetheless present. I use all my tools to combat this. I meditate before leaving my apartment. I listen to a relaxation tape or music. I do breathing exercises. I work out doing what I can still do, such as an exercise bike. I have to say that the anxiety is holding me back as much as the painful, physical long-term effects of HIV. All of this has been present for years now and before the exacerbating effects of eighteen months isolation due to COVID. Going out into the world after COVID made the situation more anxious also.

I work on forcing myself whenever I can to just push through it. If it is a theater meeting on a show, I go, and I speak up and make my opinion heard. I am no longer silent, but I am hurting while forging ahead. It is often a crippling anxiety.

My living room

DANGLING PARTICIPLES, PART TWO

I did not want to live right in Times Square because of the masses of tourists, but I needed to be within a short commute to the theater district. After three different Upper East Side apartments, I moved to Chelsea on West 25th to be able to do that easily. I am always going back and forth to either meetings or shows in the West 40s.

Although seemingly being well liked widely as a nice guy is great, I continue to prefer a small group of very close friends and confidantes. Through my whole life, I have had my inner circle friends, that core group of five or so who you confide in and trust completely. I much prefer a small one on one conversation to a larger group or a party. This inner circle is unbelievably important, and I feel so happy to have found this small circle who all have hearts of gold.

Many producer meetings are around a table with about thirty to fifty people in the room. As I said earlier, I very much dislike public speaking, but as time went on, I forced myself to be more vocal at these meetings and it became comfortable. I am not someone who will ever talk just to be heard, but I try to speak up when I believe there is something valuable to contribute. If everyone adhered to that philosophy, meetings would be much shorter and efficient! As time has gone on, I have taken on larger producer roles, being a lead producer and decision maker.

There is an age old saying that *"The eyes are the windows to the soul"*. As I mentioned before, I was lucky to inherit blue eyes from my mother that would turn out to be my most complimented feature. I very much use those eyes with those around me to look directly at them when speaking. Eye to eye conversations can communicate so much more than simply what is said aloud. The other person also feels heard; the most important part of conversation is listening. You can learn a lot about others by that simple, direct gaze. Combining that blue-eyed gaze with my ability to read others' energy provides a terrific start to finding new colleagues.

Mom with one of the grand babies

LOSING MY MOM

I was always a Mama's boy. I admired her fierce determination to be heard in a man's world. There are many great stories about her— my favorite was her going into the 19th hole bar at the golf club, which was for men only, and smoking a cigar. I recognized that she would do anything for her family. I understood that she gave up her career to raise us, but underneath there was resentment about that. She was the underdog, especially when it came to Dad's family because she was a non-Catholic outsider. She was my hero.

Within her extended family, she was the giver and the caretaker for so many. She paid the bills for many family members. She went to visit her mom every day for years and years when Grandma did not recognize anyone. She had us sing *Silent Night* to Grandma every Christmas because there would be a glimmer of light where Grandma would hum along. Tears all around...

Mom certainly had her weaknesses as we all do, but I spoke with her every day, and she did her best. She was very opinionated and very vocal in expressing those opinions. She could be stubborn. If she put her mind to achieving something, she always would (I may have inherited that...) Later in life, we all wished she drank a bit less—or maybe stopped at two drinks, rather than three.

Her last strong opinion was that she was going ahead to Florida at her normal time of year, despite having bad upper respiratory problems. We pleaded with her not to go, but she would have none of it. She arrived in Florida and basically went right into the hospital and wound up dying as it got very severe. I really wish we could have done anything to stop her from traveling. It kills me that she passed away alone. I have nightmares about that to this day. I also think she was so determined not to move into an assisted living facility that she simply had had enough.

My mom meant so much to me. Even though the roles had been reversed since childhood and the son looked after the parent, she still was my protector. I was inconsolable for months. The last parent going also seems to have so much significance. I had obviously been on my own for some time, but I always felt as though my parents had my back unconditionally. I do believe Mom and Dad are looking over me still, but I would give anything to speak to them again.

Me and my family

Mom and Dad's wedding photo

DISCOVERING THE ROMANTIC SIDE OF MY PARENTS

S ince my mom lived six months in Florida and six months in Ohio, we now had to clear out two houses. Some of it was hard work and very tedious, but we discovered some gems that allowed us to know so much more about our parents.

My father had come back on a furlough weekend to marry my mother during World War II. Dad was a dispatcher of aircraft from various locations in the U.S. He was married in his military uniform with his best friend as his best man.

My incredible discovery buried in a closet was a shoebox filled with letters they had sent back and forth while they were apart during the War. They wrote each other every day, but of course never knew when the other would actually receive the letter. They were hopelessly in love, and the key word at that time was "wooing." I did feel a little weird about reading their love letters after they were gone. But it made me understand a whole different exciting, lustful, tender, romantic, and sneaky side of them. They were basically hiding all this from their families because neither side approved.

So many of the letters were about their attempts to get their brothers and sisters and parents to accept their love. It was so sad to read how much this upset them.

But an equal number of letters were about what they missed doing with each other (*wink – wink*). However, it was couched in kind of Puritan terms. Now the letters are in my closet, and I am so glad I saw them writing in their youth. They weren't Mom and Dad then—they were a man and woman in love.

One of Dad's love letters to Mom

"They weren't Mom and Dad then—they were a man and woman in love."

Banff National Park. Alberta, Canada

Backpacking Trip with friends

MY BUCKET LIST OF PLACES AND EVENTS

Everyone has a list of places or events that are on their "bucket list." These are things that you absolutely need to experience. When you are not certain of the length of your life, they are even more important. I am lucky to have a lot of them checked off at various points in my life.

- **Stunning National Parks** – I had never been a camper or a backpacker. But three very experienced friends convinced me to go on an epic summer trip in August (quite a while ago) where we would spend a week each at Banff, Jasper and Glacier National Parks. We carried enough food and water for a week of hiking within each and then drove to the next one. Despite all the magnificent travels around the world, the views from high altitudes at these parks topped everything. It was freezing at night even in August, so fires and good sleeping bags were essential. My friends had me taking what for me were perilous trails, tight roping across logs over rivers—all things I would never do on my own. It was peer pressure at its best though exhilarating afterward, despite a few ridiculous injuries. We loved to play games in between long hikes. Once it was frisbee in the woods, and I ran full speed right into a large tree trying to catch one. Another time crossing a river, a branch snapped up and whacked me hard in the balls. Needless to say, that elicited laughter and teasing for days after. But overall, it was simply nature at its finest. American glory.

**A trip down the Pacific Coast
Highway with Bob Flicker**

Leaving him at Alcatraz

- **The Pacific Coast Highway** – A very good friend and I decided to drive the entire length of the Pacific Coast Highway at our own pace. We had no itinerary and took each day as it came. Just the scenery of driving along the coast made the trip worthwhile. If there turned out to be a site that warranted a detour, we would go off the path and return. Mount Rainier and Alcatraz were great detours. We drove all the way from Vancouver to Mexico, and it was breathtaking. Plenty of beach time along the way made it unbelievably relaxing.

Dragon Float, Rose Bowl Parade. Pasadena, California

- **The Rose Bowl** – Being a Big Ten fan, the Rose Bowl was the culmination of the football season for us, especially before they instituted a playoff system for a national champion. The Big Ten champion played the Pac Ten champion in a glorious setting after a parade filled with floats made out of roses. Getting to experience the Rose Bowl Parade up close was amazing. Walking up to the stadium labeled the Rose Bowl was even more so! A dream come true after watching it for years on TV!

- **The Kentucky Derby** – The pageantry surrounding the Kentucky Derby is historic—the women in huge hats, the mint juleps, the post parade to *My Old Kentucky Home*. The stands are packed at Churchill Downs, and the nation is watching while having their own parties around the country.

We didn't quite do it that way. We drove from NYC to KY the day before and had a bonfire party and slept on someone's lawn the night before. Then we got cases of beer and carted them into the infield for what was a mass of people going crazy with the races happening around them. On top of that, it decided to pour, so the infield became a muddy mess where college kids were sliding naked in the slippery mud. A good time was had by all. I don't know what horse won…. Or how we left…

Mardi Gras in New Orleans, LA

- **Celebrate Mardi Gras in New Orleans** – This is the wildest party imaginable. Bourbon Street is completely packed with uninhibited people having a great time. It is a must attend event, even if only once. Collecting beads was an important pastime *no matter how achieved.*

Me at the US Open at Shinnecock Hills. Long Island NY

- **The U.S. Open for Golf and Tennis** – Living in NYC, these were easier to do, but still definitely bucket list items. I was able to go to the U.S. Open golf tournament at Shinnecock Hills in Long Island. Seeing the world's best golfers up close made me realize even more how talented they are (and how bad I am)! Tiger Woods as usual had monster crowds, so we did not try to follow him, but found a perch where we could see several holes at the same time and watch all the golfers go by. My friend and I never felt our golf games to be as inadequate as we did that day while drives zoomed past us with a sound we had never made.

I also made it to the U.S. Open in tennis several times as it is a quick train ride. Sitting in the big stadium for a finals match has an electricity unrivaled. It was also fun having an entire day pass earlier in the tournament and roaming the grounds to see matches on satellite courts up close.

Duke home game with Bobby Sain

- **Attend a Duke Basketball Game** – I have been a Duke basketball fan my entire life. Their basketball stadium, Cameron Indoor Stadium, is the most famous in the country, for its Cameron Crazies fans, the very small size, and how hot it gets. The fans are doing everything possible to help their team, including a lot of jumping and off-color chants and movements. I had always wanted to go to just one game there, and it is virtually impossible. But my close friend managed to get us tickets, and we got the royal tour of the campus plus seats right at midcourt for a game through an influential person on campus he knew. We even were allowed on the court after and sat on the Duke bench. It was the most amazing gift, and I will always remember how happy I was!

I have one bucket list item I still want to experience. That is attending the Academy Awards.

On strike at the hospital

MY SECOND HEALTH EMERGENCY

One night I woke up with a very sharp pain on my lower side and tremendous difficulty breathing. Given it was the middle of the night, I decided the best way to get help was to pack a small essentials bag and catch a cab to the emergency room at Mount Sinai. The cab driver saw my terrible condition and kept talking to me, checking in, and walked me up to the front check-in. Usually there is a long wait in the outside room to be brought in and seen. However, it took everything I had to just get to the check-in desk, at which point I literally collapsed on the front desk.

I swear I did not do that on purpose, but they wheeled me into the emergency room immediately for care within five minutes. The ER was absolutely packed with some people in curtained cubicles, and the aisles were also full of patients.

The nurse was very kind and kept pushing to get me sent in for tests. For a two-hour period though I was in an aisle; they had called for me but never found me!

It turned out I had three pulmonary embolisms (blood clots in my lungs) at the same time. Not good. The nurse in the ER was trying to be nice and talking to me about theater. But during the conversation, she said to me: *If you don't make it, your work will live on.* She actually said that! It was the opposite of reassuring to say the least.

Again, I was told by the doctors at the hospital that this is potentially fatal. However, I slowly started feeling better over my time there. My friends were visiting every day, and it helped so much! They kept taking me down for scans of my lungs to see the current condition. I started feeling well enough that one day when a test was twelve hours late, and I couldn't eat for the whole day, I staged a protest by sitting in the hospital hallway. I had my blanket and was sitting on the floor chanting something ridiculous, while the doctors, nurses, and guests were walking by. The nurses thought it was really funny, and no one told me to leave. They even took pictures.

As you could probably guess, I made it through this too. I was very weak for quite a while, but I felt blessed and protected by a higher being and my friends and family.

I IDENTIFY AS A FLAMINGO

That is all. I just needed you to know that!

On Film Set

LEARNING HOW TO CAPTURE A STORY ON FILM

I have always been captivated by film but had never been involved in producing one. I met a film producer who became a very close friend, and we decided to form Dominion Pictures. Our goal was to tell captivating stories via indie or small budget films.

The process of creating a film is almost diametrically opposite that of creating a play. With film, after a pre-production process, you spend about a month shooting the entire film. You can do as many takes as you need, but the goal is to capture the story in the best possible manner forever. Shooting days can be very exhausting, but it is collapsed into a relatively short time frame. It is done, will not be changed after postproduction, and is sent out into the world to be bought and seen. The film is frozen, and everyone has done their best to create the most ideal storytelling, acting, cinematography, and special effects, etc.

On the other hand, theater projects often take years getting them to Broadway. The script process is arduous, and then multiple trials of a production often take place. There may be workshops, regional productions, and a nonprofit trial. Throughout this time period, the script is being enhanced. If it is a musical, the process is even more extenuated, as you have a score, lyrics, a band, and choreography. Songs are moving in and out; lyrics are trying to advance the story; orchestrations are adapting, etc. It is not unusual for a musical to be conceived and then take over five years to get to Broadway, if it does at all. Securing a theater is also not guaranteed, given the limited availability.

Once it does arrive on Broadway, the performances are live and are different every single night. The audience may have widely vary-ing reactions, or actors may be particularly sharp one night and off another. Unknown events occur which need to be addressed real time. In other words, the show is not frozen forever. It is living and breathing, and that is certainly part of the attraction. Audiences are seeing favorite cast members up close in real time.

I have now learned many of the nuances of film after being on set multiple times. Both processes are exhilarating, but my preference is still for live theater performances. But I love constantly learning and taking on new challenges, so adding film was welcome!

"The process of creating a film is almost diametrically opposite that of creating a play."

On set with Bryan Cranston
My cameo from the movie *Wakefield*
(with Bryan Cranston) where I play a tailor

MY FILM EXPERIENCE

As you recall, my very first theater experiences were investing in *Wicked* and co-producing *Spring Awakening*. I also had a fantastic opportunity on my second film—to be one of the lead producers on *Wakefield*, starring Bryan Cranston and Jennifer Garner. The movie has a very unusual plot, as Bryan's character supposedly has suddenly disappeared from a family home life but is actually watching them from the attic of the garage. We filmed it in Pasadena, and it was my first time observing the skills of each member of the production crew. I also have a cameo in the film in a scene with Bryan, but they cut all our improvised lines. There is a reason I am a producer and not an actor….

The highlight of course was working with Bryan Cranston again, after getting to know him on *All the Way* earlier. He is a brilliant actor and an even nicer person. He is serious at his craft, but always funny and generous to a fault. Being with him on set and then at Festivals and screenings was priceless. I would do anything with him and, in fact, co-produced *NETWORK* with him as the lead actor later on Broadway.

Lazy Susan was the next film, written by and starring Sean Hayes. Sean played a very down and out Susan trying to find her way in the world. In reality, this was not a smooth production experience, and there were many controversies among the three firms producing it. It also was not as well received as *Wakefield*. Sometimes, you learn the most important lessons in the toughest times, and this one had a myriad of lessons (which I could write a whole case study on).

I also teamed up with Stargazer Films in Kentucky on some made for TV movies. These were shot on a low budget, but the professional team there worked really hard to improve scripts and to have high production values in their films. One of their partners, Anthony Del Negro, and I became close friends and that led to the next film adventure.

Anthony and Me on the Set of Exploited

EXPLOITED

My film partner Anthony had always been a fan of the horror genre and been a part of several horror films. I was not someone who loved horror films, but they are a hot commodity in the movie industry.

We decided to co-write a psychological thriller that has horror elements but is not a classic horror film with blood and gore. *Exploited* is set on a college campus with a hacker stalking a very sexy and talented group of actors playing students. It has murder, sex, romance, and it has mystery.

I have always loved writing, but it had always been in the form of business writing or diaries or letters. Anthony and I wrote two drafts of treatments for the film and then plunged into writing. It was a total blast! The plot is quite complicated, and it required many discussions among us and the other partners. This was creativity in a form I had never been part of before. I loved the collaborative phone calls where new ideas popped up!

Shooting it was unbelievably fun. The young cast all bonded together and with us amazingly.
We were a team in every sense, and the cast threw themselves into difficult scenes. We kept on schedule and under budget—the exact opposite of the prior film. Anthony and I also were the lead producers and on set every day. We would discover while filming, that certain scenes did not really work, and we were tasked by the director to write something immediately on set. I loved that!

The whole film was shot in fourteen days in Louisville, and they were among the most fun days ever.

On the set of The Nana Project

Robin Givens directing Mercedes Ruehl, Nolan Gould and Will Peltz

DEVELOPING NEW FILM AND THEATER PROJECTS

E*xploited* was a new step, which I hope to continue to pursue with Anthony. In fact, our next film together was a heartwarming comedy loosely based on his Nana, played by Mercedes Ruehl. The film is in a mockumentary style and is called *The Nana Project*. Filming was in May 2022.

What's next? I have quite a lot to keep me busy:

- I am developing a studio feature film based on an incredible real-life story in pre-Nazi Europe with an Oscar winning writer.

- A documentary on the proliferation of guns in America is in the works.

- A new play is also in advanced writing stages, featuring three major stars.

Being somewhat behind the scenes as a co-producer on theater is a far cry from being in the middle of the action. That is also why I am taking on theater projects now as a lead producer responsible for all decisions, as opposed to one of many co-producers. The greater the involvement, the more creative passion!

"I found out I had Covid in January 2021, despite being unbelievably cautious and not going out at all."

ENTER A GLOBAL PANDEMIC

Broadway and film and the whole entertainment world in general were rolling along in a wonderful boom time when suddenly in one fell swoop it all shut down immediately on March 12, 2020. We were two days away from opening a new play and nine days from opening a musical revival of *Company*. Covid had reached the United States, and the whole country entered a full year quarantine and shutdown. Everyone suffered in their physical and mental health or through trying to maintain their financial well-being.

A full year plus of total quarantine is extremely difficult in so many ways. Everyone felt alone, isolated, scared, lonely, and missed hugs more than ever. It is estimated the pandemic has caused over one million deaths in the United States alone as of this writing. The effects of it, even on those who survived, were extreme when they caught it.

I found out I had Covid in January 2021, despite being unbelievably cautious and not going out at all. It was diagnosed two days after I went to the dentist for an emergency sharp tooth pain. My effects, with everything that had already hit my body, were totally debilitating; I had a very high fever, body aches so bad I struggled to even get out of bed, chills, severe headache, cough and congestion. It lasted about a month until everything had gone away. I was never on a ventilator though, and I do not seem to have long term effects, as some of my friends do. The long-term psychological effects of being alone for such a long period of time are significant though.

Yet another struggle, but in this case, a struggle as part of a global pandemic. Of course, my livelihood of theater and film, along with so many others, did not exist as of March 2020 and did not start up until September 2021.

The Queen's Six music ensemble

THE QUEEN'S SIX—Direct from Windsor Castle

A Full Circle Back to A Cappella Music

By total random coincidence, I met the managers of the incredible a cappella group, The Queen's Six, the day after I was amazed by their breathtaking singing at Prince Philip's funeral. They are famous in London through representing the royal family but had not been "properly" introduced to America. I was asked to join the management group to set up concerts at a famous venue and also to pursue a Broadway run for them. They have designated times when they can be on their own, unless there is a wedding or funeral or event. This new venture, bringing me back into music (not to mention an a cappella group), is *very* exciting to me! This hopefully will be a lengthy relationship.

Based at Windsor Castle, the members of The Queen's Six make up half of the Lay Clerks of St George's Chapel, whose homes lie within the Castle walls. This rare privilege demands the highest musical standards, as they sing regularly for the Royal family at both private and state occasions. In 2018 this included the wedding of Prince Harry and Meghan Markle, held in St George's Chapel and recently Prince Phillip's funeral. Most significantly, however, it is the familiarity of living and singing together in Chapel every day that lends this group its distinctive closeness and blend, as well as an irresistible informality and charm.

The Queen's Six repertoire extends far beyond the reach of the choir stalls: from austere early chant, florid Renaissance polyphony, lewd madrigals, and haunting folk songs to upbeat jazz and pop arrangements. Their vast recording projects include traditional hymns, a CD of Christmas music (originally released as the cover CD for BBC Music Magazine in 2015) along with an album of British folk songs. Recent tours include the group's trips to Greece, Slovenia, Croatia, and Bermuda.

They released their album "From Windsor with Love" on Valentine's Day, 2022, comprised of contemporary pop classic hits. This will be followed by an A Cappella Broadway album slated for release in 2023. Plans are underway for upcoming performances in New York City and a full introduction of this prestigious group to America!

"Now you have your perfect Valentines Day date for 2023 at Town Hall, New York. (Always promoting)"

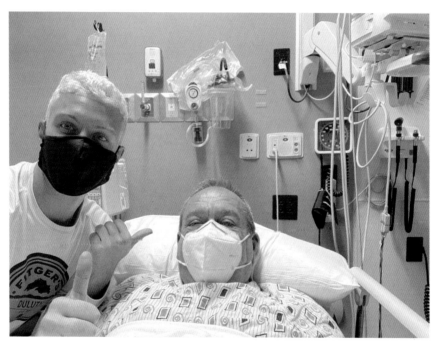

Shall we go to the hospital again?

INCARCERATED? MY LATEST LIFE THREATENING EXPERIENCE

Just very recently, I was heading down to Kentucky to film our feature film *The Nana Project*. As I walked through the airport I semi-collapsed from the very long walks, necessitating an EMT and a wheelchair. I had been proofreading the manuscript on the plane since we were about to go to print.

After I got to the hotel, I realized that I was in a lot of pain which was different from any pain I had experienced before. Thankfully, my friend insisted on getting me to the local Emergency Room right away and it probably saved my life. After a CAT scan the doctors discovered that my bladder was "incarcerated" inside a bad hernia. This was a totally different use of the word "incarcerated." I didn't know I could put my bladder in jail!

They immediately rushed me into the operating room. If the bladder was strangled to death, it could quickly result in other organ failure and gangrene. We had luckily caught it in time as the surgeon said this could have gone an entirely different way. My memoir almost became a biography! For those people who ask about my long incision in the future, the story will be that it is a bayonet wound from the Civil War– much more glamorous than the real story…

I recuperated while in a wheelchair on set for as long as tolerable each day. Everyone on set was so supportive. Although I used up one more life, it also told me that God has plans for me to do more on this planet we are destroying. And for this I am so thankful!

Mark Stager

WE ALL NEED CLOSE FRIENDS

I have said throughout my entire life that my best friends were more important than literally anything else. They have always been my personal outlet, my one-on-one bonding with total trust. I turn to my best friends with my most personal joys and failures, my most inner feelings.

I am showing a picture of one of my closest friends when I met him. He is now 73, and we are every bit as close as when I met him decades ago. (He will be upset that I am not showing his legendary cat, Maggie.)

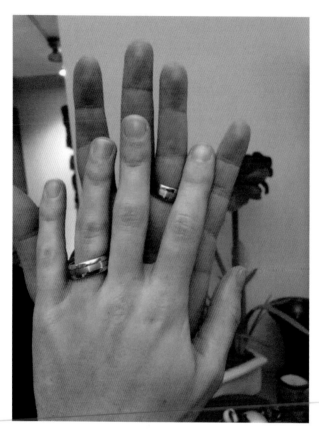

Hands and rings

ROMANTIC LOVE WILL HAPPEN WHEN IT IS LEAST EXPECTED

I have been saying so far that I am content with my constant and true friends and my life in theater, film, TV, and music. I had given up on finding a partner. Maybe that is when you find one, because he suddenly arrived in my life.

We have been together for almost six years now, and I have never felt so loved or so blessed. We have exchanged rings and vows and are always there for each other in good times and in bad times. We call each other "forever husbands."

My husband is the most kind, loving, giving man I have ever met. He is very intelligent, and everyone likes him on film sets and in everyday life. He and I can be serious one moment and incredibly goofy together the next. He constantly makes me smile and laugh. It doesn't hurt that he is incredibly good looking, but I love him for his beautiful soul.

We are both in the entertainment world and can share our love of film and theater and music. For his privacy purposes, I am not sharing his name or photo, but he is my rock. I am the luckiest man in the world to have found him! Intimacy and connection are what it is all about.

I Will Always Love You. The love of my life.

NYC Skyline from my roof

EVERY MORNING AT 6 A.M.

I have turned my waking up incredibly early into a morning ritual that puts me in such a fantastic mood to start every day. It opens my heart and opens my creative thoughts.

This is also partly the result of our quarantines during the Covid crisis. I had unsuccessful foot surgery five months before the Covid lockdown, so I was isolated for eighteen months. One of my sole reliefs from missing my friends and my Broadway and film life is my early morning time on the roof. Being alone is difficult both physically and even more so mentally.

My building has a rooftop with fantastic views of the Hudson River all the way down to the Statue of Liberty and Wall Street or up to Midtown. I go up and sit in a rocking chair and meditate with breathing exercises to be present in the moment. Meditation has become an important healing tool for me whenever I need to take a break and be in the moment. Then I pray, but in the form of Thank You to God rather than Requests to God. Thank you for keeping my family and friends safe and protected and healthy. Thank you for the smiles and laughs from yesterday.

Then I recite many times a few affirmations:
I feel peace.
I feel happy.
I feel healthy.
I feel calm.
I feel loved.
I feel blessed.

That leads me to think about all my blessings and everything I am thankful for. I thank God for making these affirmations true also for my closest friends. I direct the affirmations outward. It fills my heart. I am especially thankful for my husband and my closest friends and my brother.

The last part of my rooftop morning is open to what flows into my now much clearer head that day. Some days I marvel at the cloud patterns, the sun, and the water below me. I listen to the birds flying close by. I really love to sit silently and feel the breezes hitting me; I have always thought they are whispers from God. Whenever I am in nature, whether on a beach or in the woods or hiking, I always am aware of the breezes.

Finally, often my thoughts turn to what is to come. During this quiet time, I have the best insights on scripts and current projects. I can make clear decisions on what films or shows will excite me the most. I don't need anything more in life than my creative outlets and the love around me.

I like to say that when I do pass away, I only want the engraving on my tombstone to say: "Carl was a good friend to many."

Tulips on the roof deck in NYC

THANK YOU

Thank you for listening to my story of transformations. I realize that my story is just one of many about overcoming obstacles, by adapting my path to allow me to survive and even to thrive. The journey has led to tremendous joy in the midst of pain, if that makes sense to you also. Here it is in a nutshell:

Who I Was	Who I Adapted to
Naive Midwestern boy	Fast paced Wall Street
Closeted or unacknowledged	Gay and proud of who I am
Very healthy and active	Living with HIV/AIDS for 40 years
Surviving near death	Newfound spirituality to heal
Blank slate after pneumocystis & very low immune helpers	Listening to God and a golden bird to find a new path
Investment Banking/Consulting	Prolific theater producer and film producer
Debilitating effects of long term AIDS, blood clots, covid, immobility, lipodystrophy, anxiety, depression, more surgeries	Accepting the new reality and persevering
Finding a core group of friends with hearts of gold	Adding true love to that inner circle of true confidantes

EPILOGUE

I SINCERELY BELIEVE
WE ARE ALL HERE FOR A REASON.

I don't know why I was saved or spared from AIDS, multiple blood clots, Covid and multiple surgeries when so many others were not. What I do know is that life is not about accomplishments or power or money or awards or promotions.

We are here for much more significant reasons:

- We are here to express and receive unconditional love.
- We are here to show kindness and to do unto others as we expect them to do unto us. (I think someone wise wrote that before me...)
- We are here to make true connections with others.
- We are here to find our authentic selves deep inside and to let that self shine out to the world.
- We are here to really listen—to friends, to colleagues, to God in a breeze or on the banks of the Loire—or a seemingly magical bird.
- We are here to be out in nature and witness the unbelievable magical beauty around us.
- And we are here to not only have dreams, but to believe in them and to never give up until we have achieved them, against all odds.

"Lord, help me remember that nothing will happen to me today that you and I can't handle together."

—Anonymous

"My goal is to make audiences feel
inspired, transformed, thoughtful or
joyous through telling great stories."
—CARL MOELLENBERG

Scan the QR code to find other
amazing adventures and more from
www.ImagineAndWonder.com